AN
OPEN
LETTER
TO THE
CHURCH

On Faith, Holiness, and Being Full of the Holy Ghost

AN OPEN LETTER TO THE CHURCH

On Faith, Holiness, and Being Full of the Holy Ghost

10th Anniversary Edition

Jeanita Jinnah

Nayla Book Publishers
Michigan

Nayla Book Publishers
P.O. Box 80714
Lansing, MI 48908
naylabookpublishers.com

An Open Letter to the Church
Copyright © 2014, 2024 by Jeanita Jinnah

All Scripture quotations, unless otherwise noted, are taken from the *Holy Bible: King James Version*®. KJV®. Copyright © 1976 by Thomas Nelson, Inc. All rights reserved. Other quotations are from the following sources: New American Standard Bible (NASB). The MacArthur Study Bible. Copyright © 2006 by Thomas Nelson, Inc. The Amplified Bible (AMP). Copyright © 1987 by The Zondervan Corporation and the Lockman Foundation. All rights reserved.

All rights reserved.
No part of this book may be reproduced, scanned, or distributed in any printed or electronic form without permission. Please do not participate in or encourage piracy of copyrighted materials in violation of the author's rights. Purchase only authorized editions.

Paperback ISBN 978-0-9863889-0-3
eBook ISBN 978-0-9863889-1-0

To Ahmed,
A heart never forgets.

CONTENTS

Dedication v

Introduction ix

Section 1 Full Of The Holy Ghost

Chapter 1 Living the Spirit-Filled Life 3

Chapter 2 Acts of the Apostles 11

Chapter 3 Desire Spiritual Gifts,

But Be Careful What You Ask For 23

Chapter 4 Jesus is our Pattern 29

Chapter 5 Can These Bones Live? 37

Chapter 6 Ask God to Restore the Power 41

Section 2 Holiness

Chapter 7 Be Ye Holy, For I Am Holy 51

Chapter 8 Holiness 101 67

Chapter 9 Israel's Training in Holiness 81

Chapter 10 Israel's Dietary Restrictions 89

Chapter 11 Israel's Sacrifice 101

Chapter 12 What God Expects From Us Today 115

Chapter 13 Holiness Training Begins Immediately 121

Chapter 14 Spiritual Food and Spiritual Famine 129

Chapter 15 A Significant Sacrifice 139

Chapter 16 The Church 151

Chapter 17 Marriage 181

Chapter 18 Sex and Dating 207

Chapter 19 Letter to the Roman Church 229

Chapter 20 Letter to the Thessalonian Church 237

Chapter 21 Letter to the Corinthian Church 247

Section 3 Faith

Chapter 22 What is Faith? 263

Chapter 23 Barriers to Faith 269

Chapter 24 The Road to Faith 293

Chapter 25 Jesus' Faith in Action 309

Chapter 26 Great Faith! 321

Chapter 27 If the World Doesn't Believe 327

Chapter 28 What Would Happen If? 333

Chapter 29 My Wake-Up Call 341

Bible Study and Reflection 379

Resources 405

INTRODUCTION

It was a few years ago, when I first began to notice that something was wrong in the church. Something was missing. Today's church, in my opinion, does not look anything like the early church. The early church walked in great power and anointing. There were visible miracles, signs, and wonders that followed the preaching of the gospel. People became thoroughly convinced of the reality of God through the many works He performed through the church, and wanted to know more about Him. It was clearly evident to them that God was working through His church because they saw the physical evidence.

Many people were healed of sicknesses and diseases when hands were laid on them. Many were also freed from demonic possession and oppression when these early believers rebuked the demons in the name of Jesus, commanding them to come out. These men and women of the early church boldly proclaimed the Gospel of Jesus Christ, which has the power to save souls and to change lives. The world, through the preaching of the gospel, and the visible signs that followed, received a powerful revelation of the kingdom of God, which Jesus preached.

Not only does today's church not visibly display the same power and anointing of the first-century church, but it also does not appear to have any of the same characteristics of the first-century church. Let's face it, most Christians today are just downright mean, carnal, hateful, and self-righteous. The first-century church showed great love for humanity in their unwavering devotion to preaching the gospel, and in warning the world of the coming destruction should they not repent.

Today, we seem to focus less on the present condition of the unsaved world and more on securing for ourselves titles, positions, and the praise of men. Our churches are often a monument to ourselves, rather than to God. Sure, there are some good churches today that are working hard to evangelize the world and to win the lost for Christ. But a good majority of our churches have lost focus, and their whole reason for existing is to leave a lasting monument for themselves on this earth.

God's kingdom is not of this earth. It is spiritual and eternal in the heavens. This earth will one day pass away, but God's kingdom will live on for eternity. To become a part of God's eternal kingdom we must focus on spiritual things, where moth and rust does not corrupt *(Matthew 6:19-21)*.

I love reading the accounts of the revivals of the early 20th century in America and in Wales—the *Azusa Street Mission and Revival*, and the *Welsh Revival*. Reading the testimonies and news reports of the *Azusa Revival*, which occurred in Los Angeles, California from 1906 through 1909, awakens your senses and gives you a momentary glimpse into the workings of the Holy Ghost in our times.

During this revival, people were awakened for the first time to the power of God as He began to pour out His Spirit on all flesh, filling them with the Holy Ghost, performing miracles, signs, and wonders—similar to the New Testament Church in the book of Acts.

The believers in Los Angeles had never experienced anything quite like this before, as they had, prior to this time, not yet become acquainted with the fullness of God's power. So to know that God still performs mighty works in the earth through His children gave them a renewed hope as they began to experience Him in new ways.

These men and women were hungry for a move of God; their desire for the infilling of the Holy Ghost was great. And God does not disappoint; because, where there is a genuine hunger and longing for Him, He shows up and pours forth out of His Spirit into the hearts of the sincere seekers. And according to the reports that we have from this time, He pours out mightily.

I am fascinated by the testimonies of the *Azusa* worshipers who experienced this refreshing, or spiritual awakening. They had a front-row seat to the power of the living God. This awakening changed their lives forever. They were never, nor could they ever, be the same again.

There are accounts of people being slain under the power of God, sometimes for hours. They were unable to stand under the power of God as He began the process of remaking them into His image, through the power of the Holy Ghost. Some said that when they saw themselves in the light of God's glory they became as grasshoppers—insignificant, of little worth, and weak.

When the Spirit of God comes into a person—in His fullness—they are stripped of all pride, and filled to overflowing with great love. They have a burning desire to evangelize the lost, help the weak, and comfort the brokenhearted. Indeed, a change takes place when we are filled to overflowing with God's Spirit.

Some of the *Azusa* worshipers sought the Lord for days, weeks, sometimes months, to receive their promised blessing—the gift of the Holy Ghost, with the evidence of tongues *(See Acts 2, 10, and 19)*. According to these worshipers, it wasn't until they fully surrendered to God that He answered their prayers and filled them with His Spirit. Once they had fully died to self, God came in and did the rest. The preachers were often the last and hardest to die, according to one fellow-preacher. Because, as he put it, they were filled with too much pride so they often had a harder time humbling themselves and surrendering completely to God.

These believers were hungry for revival. They often

felt cold in their faith and distant from God. They needed a refreshing in their souls. They had read in the book of Acts how God moved through the church, performing many miraculous acts by their hands. They knew from these biblical accounts that they were not serving a dead, powerless God, and wanted to experience Him in all of His fullness.

Because of this great desire, these early 20th-century believers began to pray fervently, night and day, for God to rain down His power on them. Their strong desire for revival often led to them praying like this sometimes for years. They were consistent in prayer, determined to pray until God finally answered and released His power on the earth.

Are you desperate for a move of God in your life, in the life of your family and friends, or in your land? Are you consistent in praying for it? Are you willing to pray for days, weeks, months, or years until you receive an answer from God?

This, I believe, is what's missing in the church today. We need a spiritual awakening to revive us back to life. We have become lukewarm, much like the church at Laodicea *(see Revelation 3)*; we're neither cold or hot. We need God to pump new life into us through His Spirit. The church needs to be full of Holy Ghost power.

When God fills us to overflowing with His Spirit, we'll start to look like Him, talk like Him, and act like Him, surrendering our whole hearts to Him in service.

When we become full of the Holy Ghost, no one will have to tell us to love our neighbor because the God of love, who lives inside of us, will change our nature so that we become filled with His love. When we're full of the Holy Ghost and power, no one will have to tell us to be holy because the Holy Ghost will lead us into holiness and right-standing with God. When the church becomes full of the Holy Ghost, the world will see a change in us and know that we serve the true and living God.

It's time for the people of God to become full of God's Spirit!

The early church was fully empowered by God to perform miracles, signs, and wonders. They laid hands on the sick—and the sick were healed. They rebuked and cast out demons, setting people free of demonic oppression and possession. Paul was given handkerchiefs to pray over, which were then laid on the sick, and they were healed. People were healed by Peter's shadow passing by. Peter and Paul were full of the Holy Ghost.

Because the Lord empowered the church with Holy Ghost power, people were delivered and set free, no longer under the devil's control. Unfortunately, we see scores of people today who are still oppressed and controlled by Satan because the church is not walking in the fullness of God's power. We must have faith in the power of Jesus Christ to set people free.

The Gospel of Jesus Christ has power to change lives. When people believe in Jesus, and in the message of the cross with their whole heart, their lives are changed. Jesus does not wish to see people remain in darkness; He wants to set them free so they can walk in the light — His light.

We must not cease to preach the Gospel of Jesus Christ. There are many things being preached today: the *Gospel of Grace*, the *Gospel of Love*, and the *Gospel of Faith*; but we cannot leave out the *Gospel of Jesus Christ*.

"For it is the power of God unto salvation to every one that believeth; to the Jew first, and also to the Greek" (*Romans 1:16*). Jesus sacrificed His life so that the world might be saved. The world needs to know this. And if they don't hear it from the church, how will they hear?

We have been entrusted with the gospel. It was not given to us to hide in a box under the bed. The gospel was given to us so that we might share it with everyone who has a listening ear, and a willing heart. When Jesus returns, will He find that we have kept the gospel hidden, or will He find us boldly proclaiming the word of God to every creature throughout the world? Will He find that we have been faithful stewards over what He has entrusted to us; or will He find us consumed with carnality, strife, jealousy, envy, and pride?

Be watchful, and pray without ceasing, because no one knows the day or the hour when Christ will return to rapture His church. But, when He returns, make sure you're ready.

The Holy Ghost is a keeper; He keeps us from sinning against God, if we obey His voice. When we are full of the Holy Ghost, we will be led into holiness, and His Spirit will keep holy and sacred all those who want to be kept. As our faith in God grows, we will be able to do great things for Him. God is calling us to greatness. He's calling us out of the mediocre and into a life full of anointed power from God.

Because some believers are still carnal and have not learned to walk after the leading of the Holy Ghost, they often have to be reminded of what God expects of His children; we sometimes have to be taught how to walk upright before God, and that we have a duty to keep our temples clean and sin-free. It is for this reason that I have written this book: to be a guide to believers everywhere who desire to please God in holiness; to show them that it is possible to crucify the flesh, and keep it under subjection to God; to show believers that our faith must rise out of the ordinary and into the extraordinary, where we can do great things for God; and to show them that being full of God's Holy Spirit is the key to power in holy living.

I pray that you will use this book as a stepping stone

to becoming all that God desires you to be: holy, faithful, obedient, mature, and full of love; and that you would earnestly search God's word, and learn to rely on His Spirit to lead you into a richer, more sacred relationship with Him.

This book is broken into three sections. The first section shows us how one operates when he or she is *full of the Holy Ghost*. We read in the Bible examples of men and women who were full of God's Spirit, and God was able to use them to change lives and to preach the gospel to the ends of the earth. God also wants us, today, to experience this same power; He wants us *full of Holy Ghost power!* so that we can continue this work that the early church started. God will work together with us confirming His word through the many miracles He performs through us.

Next, we look at *holiness*, which is God's requirement for every believer. The first part of this section looks at what God expected of Israel in holiness, and the next half looks at what God expects of us today in holiness. When God delivered Israel out of Egypt, He began immediately showing them what His expectations were of them. They were no longer slaves (bound by an evil slave master) who served other gods, practiced heathen rituals, and lived under a corrupt and wicked system. They were now free (set free by a loving and holy God) and were to put away their idolatry, be holy (sacred, clean), and live and operate according to God's rules and standards, which are holy.

Holiness carries over into every area of our lives: It starts with an emotional, mental, and spiritual detachment from the world (the heart), causing us to become emotionally, mentally, and spiritually attached to God. When this attachment to God takes place, it will reflect in the way we love God and people, and in the way we honor Him with our lives, which are lived sacrificially for Him in obedience and service. We begin to act like Him, talk like Him, think like Him, and love like Him. Holiness places a distinction between God's people and the world. Holiness is God's way.

And finally, we look at a subject that is near and dear to me: *faith*. Faith is something that often appears elusive to us. We hear about people who had great faith, and the Bible tells us that we must have faith, but we usually don't know how to grab a hold of faith and apply it to our lives. This book will get you on the right road to faith. It will show you that faith is attainable, and will give you the foundation you need to walk in faith, making faith a reality in your life, no longer this elusive thing reserved for the few.

I have intentionally included a lot of Scripture references in this book because I strongly believe that the believer's life should be centered around the word of God. The word of God is like a lamp unto our feet, lighting the path, and leading the way to right-standing with God. The Bible is our instruction manual, and should be the first thing we reach for when we seek answers for how to maneuver through life's problems, and how to live spiritually-sound lives. All the answers we need that pertain to life and godliness are found in the Bible. If it's not in the Bible it's not truth, no matter how strongly we believe something. God's word is truth, and it is our source. Use it wisely.

I would also encourage you to use the *study guide* in the back of the book as a tool to lead you into a more thorough study of God's word. This would be excellent for either a personal study, a small group study, or for Christian Education. It is important for believers to know and understand what "thus saith the Lord" so that we know what God expects of us, and how to please Him. Also, the word of God grants us access into the mind and the heart of God. What better way to get to know a person than to read about them in *their own words.* When we read and study the Bible, we become closer to God as He draws closer to us through His holy word. If you want to know what God thinks of you, study His word!

We truly serve an awesome and powerful God. Our God is not dead; He is alive, and He wants to use us to do great things for the kingdom. But we must be filled with His Spirit, and walking in faith. If you want to walk in the same power and anointing as the church in the book of Acts, and experience the same refreshing that the believers at the *Azusa Mission* experienced, you must die to self, and allow God to fill you to overflowing with

His Spirit. This power is what the church needs today in order to fulfill our mission here on earth: spreading the Gospel of Jesus Christ to the ends of the earth so that the lost might hear, believe, and be saved.

SECTION 1

FULL OF THE

HOLY GHOST

רוח קדושה
HOLY GHOST

Chapter 1

LIVING THE SPIRIT-FILLED LIFE

The Bible makes a point of bringing to our attention when a person is *full of the Holy Ghost*. For example, Stephen, who was murdered for the witness of Jesus Christ, was a man full of the Holy Ghost. In fact, right before he was murdered, witnesses said he had the face of an angel. This is also where the now Apostle Paul, then Saul, comes into the picture. He was consenting to

Stephen's death, and in fact, kept the coats of those who murdered him.

Stephen preached a divinely-inspired message on the divinity of Jesus Christ that was hard for the Jews to refute, and pleaded with them to believe in this Jesus, and to follow Him. I'm sure these people could see the anointing of God on Stephen's life and were probably jealous of him because of it. But because their hearts were hardened and they were blinded by sin, they did not receive his message, and stoned him to death. As he was dying, Stephen asked God to forgive them, and prayed for God to receive his spirit into heaven. His was not a life wasted. He was a martyr for Jesus, and his legacy still lives on. Stephen was a testament of a life lived in service to God, of one who lived a Spirit-filled life, and one who was willing to suffer for the sake of the kingdom.

James, the brother of Jesus, was reported to be a man of prayer. It was said of him that he prayed so much that his knees were like a camel's knees, rough and hardened by time spent on them in prayer and devotion to God. James likely grew up in the same house as Jesus, and they were raised as brothers. I'm sure he was blessed by his close proximity to Jesus, and by having had a front-row seat to the character and the divine-like nature of Jesus, and having witnessed the many miracles He performed during His brief, but powerful ministry. James saw Jesus' devotion to God in prayer and service, and came to believe on Jesus as the Son of God, the Messiah who was to come and take away the sins of the world. He must have patterned himself after Jesus' prayer life, service, and devotion to God.

James is reported to be the author of the book of James, who tells us that our faith in Jesus must produce works. If our faith in Jesus Christ does not have corresponding deeds and acts of obedience to back it up, it is dead. Our faith must produce fruit.

When we are full of Holy Ghost power there will be clear, unmistakable signs. These signs show that what we are proclaiming to be the Gospel of Jesus Christ is fully co-signed and backed up by the full force and power of the living God.

We, therefore, have to stay in constant communication with God: in prayer often, fasting much, which helps us crucify the flesh; and we must commit time to devotion and to Bible study.

We must learn to crucify the flesh and to be sensitive to the Spirit, being led by the Spirit. Pray also for discernment, but use it wisely, and prayerfully. Don't use it to be nosy or a busybody, or to look down on people with contempt when God shows you something about a person's spirit and/or motives. But, pray for that person, because this could be the reason God is showing you these things.

The person who is full of God's Spirit must be a willing vessel, and cannot be filled with pride. In other words, you must be humble. Moses was said to be a very humble man—more humble than any man on earth. He valued spending time in God's presence, where God taught him and molded him to do the work He had called him to do. God trained Moses, and raised him up for greatness. There was no one in the whole world like Moses.

Paul was a man who came to be hated by the Jews. He suffered many trials for the gospel's sake *(2 Corinthians 11:23-27)*. He went from being loved by the elite to being hated by them for turning to follow this Jesus, whom he once persecuted. When the Jews heard that Paul was now a follower of Jesus, they immediately began to conspire to kill him. This is often the life of a servant of God. It's not always an easy life, but it is one that will be rewarded in the end if you remain faithful to Him.

William J. Seymour spent several hours a day in prayer, and God used him to preside over the *Azusa Revival* and the early 20th century reawakening of the Spirit of God in the lives of believers in California, its surrounding areas, and eventually around the world. Pastor Seymour was reported to be a very humble man. The services at the *Azusa Street Mission* were well-reported around the world for their powerful manifestations of God's power. People came from around the world to experience God, and to receive their baptism in the Holy Ghost, with the evidence of speaking in tongues. These people would then travel the world sharing their testimonies of what God was doing at *Azusa*, and leading others into their own spiritual awakening to the power of God.

When the early church was in search of men who could be trusted to look over the distribution of food and aide to the widows, the Apostles told the church to search for men who were honest, and full of the Holy Ghost and wisdom, and place them over this responsibility. They eventually chose seven men who met these qualifications; Stephen was among the seven. Stephen stood out because he was a man full of faith and power, and the Lord performed great miracles and wonders through him. The people took note of this extraordinary power, became jealous of him, and eventually had him stoned to death.

The men and women who are mentioned in the book of Acts were full of faith, and filled with God's Holy Spirit. The Lord worked through them to perform His will on the earth. These men and women were the instruments God used to spread the Gospel of Jesus

Christ, break Satan's chains of bondage over people's lives, heal the sick and afflicted, and bring God's kingdom to earth to be experienced by all.

These individuals were not necessarily extraordinarily gifted, or from among the elite classes of society, nor were they the wisest. They were actually men and women just like you and I, who had regular jobs, families, and were your normal ordinary, hardworking people. But God saw something in them, and He chose them to be carriers of the gospel, and to place His anointing upon them. (We will look more closely at the book of Acts in the next chapter.)

God's anointing is given to us to advance His ultimate goal of restoring man back to God so that none are lost. This was Jesus' reason for coming to earth, and ultimately dying for the sins of the world. And this should also be the church's mission: to see that God's goal is accomplished.

In order for the church to accomplish this goal, we must separate ourselves from the world. Although we are in the world, we are no longer a part of the corrupt worldly-system. We must be transformed by God into His heavenly kingdom, sanctified, and set apart for the master's use.

Through Jesus, God has rescued us from darkness, and transferred us into the kingdom of His beloved Son, in whom we have redemption and forgiveness of sins. Our fates have been sealed, and the devil can't snatch us out of God's hands, but *we* can relinquish our seats by turning away from God, and back to embrace a life of sin. Remain firmly planted in God's kingdom; allow Him to fill you up with His Spirit, which keeps you in right relationship with God, and leads you into all truth. The Spirit will never lead us outside of the will of God.

Chapter 2

ACTS OF THE APOSTLES

We see the Holy Ghost at work in the book of Acts as He works through the followers of Jesus, performing many miraculous acts. The Holy Ghost filled the void that Jesus left when He ascended back up to heaven. He stood in as Jesus' replacement. He became that Comforter for these early believers that Jesus had once been to them. The Holy Ghost was now their teacher, providing further instructions in godliness, and teaching them how to please God in holiness. He empowered these believers to duplicate the acts Jesus performed through the power of the Holy Ghost, which He received from the Father. Jesus' followers were empowered by the Holy Ghost to finish the work He started here on earth. The disciples were to continue to spread the gospel to the ends of the earth, leading a lost and dying world to reconciliation with the Father.

These men and women were our predecessors, and set an example for us to follow of how a disciple of Jesus Christ should conduct himself, utilizing the power and anointing of God. They show us how to remain faithful to God in the midst of persecution, and how to testify of the divine nature of Jesus, as He often testified to them of God, and of His relationship to the Father.

Just as Israel's disobedience to God in the wilderness was written as an example, or warning, to us of how *not* to behave towards God, the accounts written in the Book of Acts of the saints' empowered lives, and acts of obedience to Jesus, were written as an example for us to follow of how to live a Spirit-filled life, as we are directed by the Holy Ghost. We should read these stories, study them, and allow the Holy Ghost to direct us as He directed the lives of the first-century church. Open up your mind, and your heart, and allow the Holy Ghost to lead you, and to use you for God's glory.

God's will is that His church is anointed with power from Him, and that we live a Spirit-filled life, which will empower us to rise above our circumstances, not being overpowered by the devil, who is the god of this world. God's power is greater than any other power, and as His children, we have access to this power; we must, therefore, use it wisely.

> PRAYER IS A VERY IMPORTANT PART OF THE CHRISTIAN LIFE.

Prayer is a very important part of the Christian life. God moves through prayer. When we are persistent in prayer, a portal opens up to heaven, and God begins to perform mighty works among, for, and by His people.

The disciples continued on one accord through

prayer and they received their promised Pentecost—the infilling of the Holy Ghost, with power. On another occasion, the disciples were on one accord in prayer all night for Peter, who had been imprisoned by King Herod. And in response to the prayers, God sent an angel to deliver Peter from prison.

Also, how can we forget about Paul and Silas, who were not discouraged by their chains, but began to pray and sing songs all night, when God shook the prison with power loosing them from their bonds and opening the prison doors. This manifestation of God's power caused the jailer to believe, repent, and be baptized, along with his whole house.

What are you doing that would cause God to send His angel to deliver you from your prison—whatever it may be. Are you boldly proclaiming the name of Jesus Christ? Are you teaching and preaching repentance and deliverance from sin in His name? Are you faithful in prayer, believing that God will do what you are asking Him to do? When prayer goes up, God's power is made manifest through the many miracles He performs in response to these prayers.

When we are full of the Holy Ghost, our faith reaches up to heaven and brings heaven down to earth, and God's will is performed on earth, as it is in heaven. When God fills us up with His Spirit, we are removed of all pride and doubt, which can stand in the way of the blessings God desires to give to us. When we are filled up with God, we are emptied out of ourselves. We are limited to what we can do on our own in the natural, but there are no limits or barriers for a Spirit-filled believer who is sold out for God. Miracles, signs, and wonders follow the Spirit of God.

Peter and John, being full of the Holy Ghost, made their way to the temple for prayer. There, by the gate of the temple, which is called Beautiful, lay a man who had been lame from birth. This man was carried daily to the gate to beg for money. I'm sure Peter and John had passed this man many times before on their way to the temple; but this day was different. When the lame man asked them for money on this day, Peter looked him in the eyes and said, *I have something better than money - I have the gift of God residing on the inside of me. In the name of Jesus Christ of Nazareth, I command you to rise up and walk.* And Peter took him by the right hand and lifted him up, and immediately, the lame man's feet and ankles received strength. And he leaped up, and stood on his own two feet for the first time, and walked. The man entered the temple, walking, leaping for joy, and praising God. Those who had for years seen him lying by the gate begging knew that they had just witnessed a miracle.

> THEY WERE FULL OF POWER AND FAITH.

Peter and John had just come out of a remarkable prayer service where everyone there had been filled with the Holy Ghost, and with power *(See Acts 2)*. They were full of power and faith and it transferred over into a lame man's life, resulting in him being healed. He was touched by the power of God.

The next day, the chief priests and elders called Peter and John forth to question them about the miracle that had occurred with the lame man who was made whole. They could not deny that this was in fact a miracle; the evidence was clear. So they tried a different tactic, threatening them and commanding them not to preach or to teach in the name of Jesus Christ. But Peter and John said, "we can't help but speak the things we have seen and heard. It is better for us to obey God rather than man." After further warnings, they let them go.

> THE SPIRIT WILL LEAD US INTO DIVINE ENCOUNTERS.

Peter was so full of the Holy Ghost that people brought the sick into the streets, laying them on beds and couches that perhaps the shadow of Peter alone passing by might overshadow them and heal them. All of these, including those who were troubled by unclean spirits, were healed.

The Spirit will lead us into what I call *divine encounters.* This is what happened to Philip when he encountered the Ethiopian Eunuch. An angel of the Lord spoke to

Philip, telling him to go down from Jerusalem to Gaza. While on his way, Philip noticed a man sitting in a chariot coming back from Jerusalem, where he had gone to worship. The Spirit told Philip to go up to the chariot; and when he did, he heard the eunuch reading from the book of Isaiah. Philip asked him if he understood what he was reading. He said, no. Then Philip began to open up the Scriptures to him, and preach Jesus. The eunuch believed, and asked Philip if he could baptize him. The two men went down to the water together, and Philip baptized him. When they came up out of the water, the Spirit carried Philip away, and the eunuch went on his way, rejoicing and praising God.

God will speak to us through His Spirit, leading us into similar situations where we can minister the Gospel of Jesus Christ to a lost soul, causing them to believe, and be baptized.

Wherever the Spirit of the Lord is, there is liberty. The church should not be comfortable seeing people bound by sin, drugs, alcohol, pornography, depression, and demonic oppression. The Holy Ghost that dwells in us should move us to act to bring about deliverance and freedom for all.

The disciples, having sat at the feet of Jesus, were moved with compassion and love for the masses. They studied Him, and patterned themselves after Him. Jesus gave them their mission, and empowered them to carry it out. The things that they did by the Spirit were fully sanctioned by God. Many people were healed of leprosy, blindness, deformities, demonic possession and oppression. Many deaf people received their hearing, and the lame were made to walk.

When the disciples laid their hands on someone, God poured out His Holy Spirit on them, and they were instantly converted. They were transformed and made brand new, as God removed them from the kingdom of darkness into His holy kingdom.

The Lord sent Ananias to Saul to lay hands on him so that he might receive his sight. While on his way to Damascus with warrants to arrest and imprison those who believed on Jesus, Saul was blinded by a bright light from heaven. God spoke to him through an audible voice—which those who were with him also heard—and told him that He had chosen him to preach the gospel to the Gentiles. Immediately, Saul was convicted of his sins, and humbled before the Lord. Subsequently, he also came to believe in and follow Jesus, and became one of His boldest and fiercest proponents. Saul turned many to Jesus through the preaching and teaching of the gospel.

Saul, now the Apostle Paul, was anointed by God to carry the gospel to the Gentiles. He preached that salvation is no longer only for the Jews, but is now available to the Gentiles as well. Salvation is through Jesus Christ, whom the world crucified. But God raised Him back to life, after three days, and placed all power in His hands. Jesus has been elevated by God and is now seated at the right hand of the Father.

Paul discipled many people, and helped establish several churches. He wrote many letters (or, epistles) to these churches, encouraging them in their faith and addressing issues as they arose in the church. We are blessed to have these divinely inspired letters today.

They grant us access into the mind of God, and His will as it relates to the church. Later, we will take a look at a few of the letters Paul wrote to the churches at Rome, Thessalonica, and Corinth: namely Romans, 1 Thessalonians, and 1 Corinthians.

The disciples' preaching and teaching led many to faith in Jesus Christ, the long-awaited Messiah. They traveled extensively throughout the region sharing the good news of the gospel, and testifying of the miracles, healings, and deliverances they had witnessed during their time with Jesus. These men were chosen by God to be witnesses of Jesus' virgin birth, His ministry, His death, His burial, and His resurrection. They witnessed God's confirmation of Jesus through an audible voice from heaven, and witnessed Him being filled with the Holy Ghost.

Peter, James, and John were present during His transformation on the mountain. When Jesus was transformed in the presence of God, His garments became white, and He conversed with Elijah and Moses. Peter, James, and John heard the audible voice from

God which thunderously declared, "This is my beloved Son; hear Him."

Jesus' disciples became convinced that He was their long-awaited Messiah, and wanted to share this belief with the world so that the world would also believe, and be saved.

The disciples exhibited for us many of the attributes of a true disciple of Jesus. A true disciple walks in the fullness of God's power; shares the gospel with the world freely; is firmly rooted in their faith, and completely devoted to God; is a mighty prayer warrior; walks in love; and has been empowered by the Holy Ghost to set people free from bondage. May we never forget the bravery and the sacrifices of the men and women who went before us.

Chapter 3

DESIRE SPIRITUAL GIFTS, BUT BE CAREFUL WHAT YOU ASK FOR

The Prophet, or man of God, didn't always have an easy life. This wasn't a coveted profession, the way it is today. These men were often ostracized, and alone. People didn't run to hear the prophet when he came to town the way people run to hear a popular preacher today, when he comes to town. (You going to hear so-and-so tonight?!) No one thought to invite the man of God over when they had gatherings at their homes. He wasn't that popular. He was usually a loner, and an outcast.

The Bible tells us to desire spiritual gifts. But, we should also understand what is required of us when we are given these gifts. Covet the best gifts to help edify the church, but understand that these gifts will not make you popular. People may even want to kill you.

John the Baptist was anointed in his mother's womb to be the forerunner of Jesus. He was chosen to prepare the way for Jesus. John was given the preaching ministry of the *baptism of repentance* to prepare the hearts of men to receive the baptism of Jesus Christ, who would save the world from their sins.

John often lived in the wilderness. He wore camel's skin, and ate locusts and wild honey. I can imagine that at times he even looked scraggly and unkempt—like a Grizzly Adams. John was a prophet of God who prophesied what God told him to speak to the people. I imagine these prophetic utterances spoke warnings and corrections into the lives of people, warning them of God's wrath if they didn't change their ways. John was unlike today's modern-day "prophets" who often only speak material blessings and positive affirmations into people's lives. Today's prophetic utterances are usually "feel good" messages that are often well received by the people.

> JOHN WAS UNLIKE TODAY'S MODERN-DAY PROPHETS.

John the Baptist boldly told King Herod that it was wrong for him to have his brother Philip's wife (Herodias). When Herodias, the evil adulteress that she was, heard this, she schemed to have John killed. When her daughter danced before the king, and his royal audience, she pleased the king, and he told her to ask for anything she wanted, up to half of the kingdom. When she went to her mother, Herodias, to ask her what she should ask for, her mother told her to ask for John the Baptist's head on a charger. When the king heard this he was grieved, but because he had promised her anything she wanted, he sent and had John beheaded in prison, and his head brought to her on a charger, which she then gave to her mother.

The Prophet Elisha is most known for the many miraculous works he performed, and for being the successor of Elijah. God told Elijah to anoint Elisha as his successor, prior to Elijah's being taken away by God in a whirlwind to heaven. When Elijah told Elisha to ask him for anything he wanted prior to his departure, Elisha said, "I want a double-portion of your spirit."

> "I WANT A DOUBLE-PORTION OF YOUR SPIRIT."

Elijah said, "you have asked a hard thing, but if you see me when I'm taken away, your request will be granted."

As you might imagine, Elisha stuck close by Elijah's side, never allowing him out of his sight for one moment. His dedication was rewarded, because, while the two were on their way to Jordan, the Lord sent a chariot of fire, being pulled by horses of fire, to take away Elijah. Elisha witnessed this, and picked up the mantle that fell from Elijah as he was ascending to heaven. Elisha's request was granted; he received a double-portion of Elijah's spirit.

Elisha was a mighty man of God. He was a prophet during the time of Ahab, the king of Israel. He and Ahab had a contentious relationship because Elisha never prophesied anything nice concerning King Ahab, who was a wicked king, along with his manipulative wife, Jezebel. God was not pleased with Ahab, and spoke through Elisha warnings for Ahab to change his evil ways. Ahab did not change his ways, and was eventually killed in battle, as Elisha had prophesied.

The office of the prophet was fraught with many hardships and perils. People often wanted to kill the prophet because they didn't like the things he prophesied concerning them. They were often ridiculed, heckled, imprisoned, beaten and left for dead. It wasn't uncommon for the prophet to have to flee for his life. This was not a desirable office, but it was necessary, because the prophets were the carriers of God's holy messages to man. They were entrusted with God's word; therefore, they took their jobs seriously.

Don't shy away from the gift of God on your life. God anoints us and equips us to do His work, and to carry His message of repentance from sin, and to forewarn the world of the wrath to come for those who refuse to turn away from sin. This work will not make us popular with the world; they will hate us because we are not of the world, nor do we cosign with their sin. Our job is not to seek to please man, but to please God.

God is looking for a few good men, and women, who are willing to be His representatives here on earth. Allow Him to fill you up with His Holy Spirit, which gives you the tools you need to represent Him well, and to carry His gospel to the ends of the earth. Desire the best gifts, and remain faithful to God.

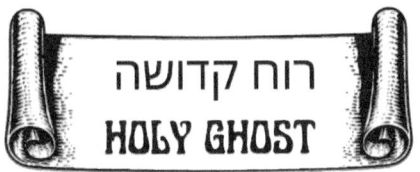

Chapter 4

JESUS IS OUR PATTERN

I love reading the accounts of Jesus' life and ministry, particularly in the book of Luke (which is my personal favorite). It was while reading this book that my spiritual eyes first began to open to God's will as it relates to healing. You see through the accounts written in this gospel that wherever Jesus went, He healed people. Everyone was healed by Him, from the leper, to the man with the withered hand, who sat in the Synagogue on the Sabbath listening to Jesus teach. The only time Jesus did not heal anyone was when they did not have the faith to be healed. He was actually disheartened by their lack of faith.

Jesus boldly declared that He came to do the will of His Father, and that everything He did was sanctioned by God. What is the will of God? To open the eyes of those who are spiritually blind and walking in darkness. To reconcile a dying world back to Himself. To heal and to set free all those who have been held captive by the devil through sickness, disease, and mental and physical bondage. God's will is for all of mankind to be saved.

> JESUS WAS OBEDIENT TO GOD, EVEN UNTO DEATH.

Jesus was obedient to God, even unto death. He was willing to sacrifice temporary earthly pleasures, and to endure sufferings in order to fulfill the mission God sent Him to earth to fulfill. Jesus knew that the sufferings He would endure here were nothing compared to the eternal glory He would enjoy in heaven, when He would be rewarded by God for His faithfulness. He also loved the world, and wanted to save it from the coming destruction - when God will pour out His wrath on the earth, and on all those who refuse to turn to Him in faith and obedience.

Jesus was a teacher. He was often called Rabbi, which means teacher. People saw Him as an authority on all things relating to God. They saw His knowledge and wisdom of the Scriptures, and sought Him out for further clarity and insight. When Jesus taught, He spoke with authority, and as one who was divinely-inspired to speak on matters of a spiritual and religious nature. Jesus was seen as a spiritual authority by many.

Jesus would go into the Synagogues and open up the Scriptures to them. He would also be seen with a crowd gathered around Him listening intently to His parables, and hanging on His every word. He imparted spiritual wisdom into those who followed after Him; He trained them, and taught them how to be His disciples. Jesus knew the importance of imparting into people's lives the things which He had received from God. This impartation opened their eyes to the wonders of God, which strengthened their faith in God, and enabled them to carry on after Jesus' departure.

Jesus was a great provider. He told Simon Peter to launch his ship out into the deep, and for him and his men to prepare for a great catch of fish. When they obeyed, they were supplied with a great catch of fish to where their nets began to break.

Jesus also provided money for His disciples to pay taxes when He told them to go to a certain place, and catch a fish. When they pulled the fish out of the water and opened its mouth, there, in the fish's mouth, was the money they needed to pay their taxes.

And, Jesus notoriously fed a multitude, on multiple occasions, with just a few fish, and a few loaves of bread. His provisions never ran out.

Demons were subject to His authority. They recognized Him as the Son of God, and often cried out to Him, or begged Him not to cast them out. When He rebuked them and commanded them to come out, they obeyed His voice and came out of the person they had possessed and oppressed, sometimes for years.

Jesus prayed often. He would often be seen going up a mountain to pray, sometimes staying there all night to spend time alone with God. During these times of prayer, I can imagine Jesus received the strength and the encouragement He needed to continue His earthly mission. God was also probably giving Him instructions and direction on how to complete this mission, and reminding Him of the things He still needed to accomplish to fulfill the Scriptures.

These times of fellowship with God were precious to Him. It was not often that He could get alone to talk to God because the crowds sought Him out, and followed Him everywhere He went. Some, out of curiosity, and others were hoping to receive something from Him, be it a free meal, or deliverance for their bodies. And there were yet others who followed Him just to find something to accuse Him of. Prayer was very important to Jesus; He even taught His disciples to pray.

Jesus was also an anointed preacher, preaching the

good news of the kingdom of God, and encouraging people to put their complete trust in God's kingdom, which is eternal in the heavens, where decay and corruption cannot touch it. For, the kingdoms of this world are temporary, corrupt, worldly, and nothing to be compared to God's holy kingdom. Jesus brought heaven to earth through the preaching of the gospel, introducing the world to a holy God who is all-powerful, loving, and full of grace and mercy, but also one who does not let the guilty go unpunished.

The gospel He preached was powerful, setting people free from oppression, and a life destined to end in destruction. It brought hope to the poor, healing to the brokenhearted, deliverance to the captives, and recovery of sight to the blind (both literally and spiritually). He taught the world how to be accepted by God.

This is something the church needs to know today: how to be accepted by God. To be accepted by God means that we are often hated by the world. The church cannot be a friend of the world. When we love the world more than we love God, we are not His disciples. When we love the world more than God, we cannot make it into His holy kingdom, because His kingdom is not of this world.

Yes, He created the world, but the world has become corrupt, unholy, and sinful. The world has turned their backs on God, desiring rather to please themselves and to live according to their own rules, disobeying God's rules. The world is an enemy of God. God seeks to redeem man, and to restore him back into His good graces. Jesus Christ is the only way back to the Father. Salvation is through Jesus Christ. The pattern has been set, and the way has been made for us to follow after Jesus. He is the way, the truth, and the life.

רוח קדושה
HOLY GHOST

Chapter 5

CAN THESE BONES LIVE?

The Spirit of the Lord carried the prophet Ezekiel away in the spirit, into a valley of dry bones. The life had long since gone out of these bones. They were strewed here and there. Even the skin had dried up and dissipated. They were now old, lifeless, dusty bones. Then, the Lord asked Ezekiel, "Son of man, can these bones live?" Ezekiel's response to the Lord was, "O

Lord God, you know."

The Lord told Ezekiel to prophesy over the dry bones; speak to the bones, tell them the Lord will cause breath to enter into them so that they may come to life. Tell them that the Lord will cause sinew (muscle, or strength), flesh, and skin to grow back over and cover the bones, causing them to come alive again. When Ezekiel began to prophesy these things over the dry bones, there was a noise, and a rattling of the bones as they began to come together, and behold, the sinew and the skin covered them, as God had said. But there was no breath, or life, in them.

> THEY WERE AN EXCEEDINGLY GREAT ARMY.

Then the Lord told Ezekiel to prophesy to the breath, telling it to come from the four winds and breathe on these that have been restored, so that life enters back into them. So Ezekiel prophesied as instructed, and the breath came into them, and they suddenly came to life and stood up on their feet. They were an exceedingly great army.

These bones signified the house of Israel. God was showing Ezekiel through this vision that although Israel was dead, He would bring them back to life, causing them to be a great nation.

I believe God also wants to restore the church back to life, just as He did in Ezekiel's vision with the dry bones. The church today has become a valley of dry bones, where no power or anointing can be detected in it. God wants us to live the Spirit-filled life, walking and operating under the power and anointing of the Holy Ghost. He wants to once again perform mighty works of miracles, healings, and deliverance through the church. God wants the dead to be restored to life, the lame to walk, the dumb to talk, and the deaf to hear. But before this can happen, we have to step out of the fleshly realm, and begin to operate in the spiritual realm through the power of the Holy Ghost. I strongly believe this is God's will for the church.

It's time for us to put away carnality, impurity, immorality, pride, and disobedience, and start living the life that we were called to live in Christ.

Can these dead bones live? I believe they can. I believe God can breathe new life into the church, reviving us, and restoring us back to life. He wants to raise us up on our feet, and cause us to be that great army Ezekiel saw in his vision. There is yet more work for us to do for Him. Time is short; Jesus is soon to come. When the church starts once again operating under the power and anointing of the Holy Ghost, great things will happen. The world will come to see and believe in God through His power manifested through His works, and the sinner will come to God asking, "what must I do to be saved?"

רוח קדושה
HOLY GHOST

Chapter 6

ASK GOD TO RESTORE THE POWER

On Sunday, December 23, 2013, we had a very bad ice storm in Michigan, which left thousands of homes without power. I had spent the weekend out of town celebrating Christmas early with my family. When I arrived home on Sunday evening, I discovered the power was out in my apartment. At the time, I knew nothing about the storm, and assumed the power would only be out for a short time. So, I decided to wait it out and hope for the best.

To ward off the cold, I spent the evening under layers of blankets, and layers of clothing. As you might imagine, there really isn't much you can do without electricity, so I mostly sat and thought, not wanting to move around too much because of the cold. I really love the quiet, because it gives me valuable time to think. And the house was very still and quiet this evening. I passed the time by occasionally checking for status updates on the power company's website on my cell phone. But, wanting to preserve my battery, I mostly kept my phone shut off.

> "ASK ME TO RESTORE THE POWER."

As the evening progressed, and as I was sitting there in the dark, I heard the Lord speak to me. He said, "Ask me to restore the power." When I heard this, I sat there for a few moments thinking about what I had just heard. Now, it might seem only natural after hearing God tell me to ask Him to restore the power that I would immediately respond, "yes Lord, please restore the power!" But I did not. As I sat there in the cold, I thought that if anyone can restore the power, God can. And I became humbled before Him.

I did not rush to ask God to restore the power because I did not want to approach Him with a sense of entitlement—as if God *owed* me something. Sometimes, as Christians we can often feel entitled, as if God *has* to move on our behalf because we are His children. But God owes us nothing. He chooses to bless us because He loves us, not because He has to. And as I sat there in the dark, I began to think about His goodness, and the grace and mercy He has shown me over the years. He's always been there for me, even when people weren't. He was even with me, carrying me through some rather dark times in my life. He has never left my side. And as I sat there on this evening thinking about all of this, a sense of thankfulness began to wash over my soul as I reminisced about the goodness of the Lord. When we approach God, we should do so

> HE HAS NEVER LEFT MY SIDE.

reverently, humbling ourselves before Him, and with a spirit of thanksgiving. This was my attitude on this evening.

Well, I did eventually ask God to restore the power. I asked Him to restore the power to my apartment, and for the people around me, because this is Michigan, in winter, and Lord, people need their power! I had seen on the power company's website that the electricity in my area was not scheduled to be restored until later that week. But I didn't let this bother me because I had already prayed asking God to restore the power.

> GOD NEVER CEASES TO AMAZE ME.

The next day, I rose up early to run some errands and to warm up a bit, as the power was still out in my apartment. Around 3:00pm, I decided to run home to see if the power had come back on. As I approached, I began to see signs of life and was very encouraged. When I walked through the front door and flipped on the light switch, there was light! God had restored the power!

God never ceases to amaze me. He cares about even

the smallest details of our lives. He's not a faraway God, who is "out there" somewhere. He's very near to us, and willing to become intimately involved in our lives. I praise God for restoring the power.

Thankfully, I only had to spend one night without power, but there were many homes throughout the city that were without power for several days. Quite a few families had to move into hotels and warming centers for the week, with most losing the contents of their refrigerators as things began to spoil. And mostly, people were just greatly inconvenienced by this storm. So, I take nothing for granted.

Later, as I began to reflect more on this incident, I began to think that maybe it wasn't just about the heat and electricity. Maybe, God telling me to ask Him to restore the power was a metaphor. Prior to this, I had been thinking a lot about the church and wondering why the church has not been walking in the fullness of God's power. Quite frankly, the church is dead.

> QUITE FRANKLY, THE CHURCH IS DEAD.

We have not seen a mighty move of God, for quite some time.

The signs that usually follow the preaching of the gospel (healing, deliverance, the dead being raised back to life), which used to be regular occurrences, are now so seldom seen, that not only do we seem to no longer expect them, but we even seem to doubt if God is still able to perform them. But, God *is* able. The church has just not been walking in the fullness of God's power. We have become spiritually dead, much like the dead bones in Ezekiel's vision. God wants to restore His power back into the church so that these signs once again manifest themselves, so that the world will know that God is All-Powerful, and begin to believe on Him, and follow after Him.

This was my prayer then, and it continues to be my prayer today: "Lord, restore the power in your church!" We need God working through us, confirming the preaching of the gospel, and saving a lost and dying world from certain destruction. God's power is real, and the church has been granted access to this power through

Jesus Christ. We are to be the conduits through which God makes Himself known to the world. Our lives should be a testimony of the existence and power of the living God.

I ask that you join me in praying that God would restore the power in the church. As we begin to expect God's supernatural power to be unleashed in the earth, then will we start to see the signs that testify to the power and ability of the living God. The world will also see and believe. Make this your prayer today, and watch God's power begin to move mightily once again on the earth.

SECTION 2

HOLINESS

קְדוּשָׁה
HOLINESS

Chapter 7

BE YE HOLY, FOR I AM HOLY

The Lord told Israel that He is a holy God, and that He also expects them to be holy. However, this statement does not begin and end with Israel; God also expects you and I to be holy. In order to live in peace and harmony with a holy God, we must lead a life that is pleasing to Him. God sets the standards for holiness, and it is up to you and I to follow and obey.

The word of God is the Christian's ultimate "instruction manual," teaching us about God; showing us how to please Him through faith and obedience; giving us examples of how we should serve Him through praise and worship; emphasizing how to be His witnesses in the earth through the preaching and teaching of the gospel; and expressing in clear terms what His expectations are for His children. A true Christian is a follower of Christ, in every sense of the word. He is not just a hearer of the word, but he hears and obeys.

While listening to Jesus teach in the temple courts, certain Jews believed on Him (that He was the Son of God). Jesus said to these believing Jews: *If you continue in my word (hold fast to my teachings, and live in accordance with them), then are you my disciples indeed.* When we hear the word and believe, we must then live in accordance with the word we've heard.

Jesus expressly shows us how to serve God: through His obedience, even unto death; by being aware of His mission, and seeing it through to completion; by putting

God's will above His own; and by showing us, through His life and example, how to live holy.

Jesus is not the exception to the rule. This same unwavering devotion to God is possible for the believer today. Jesus took on flesh and came to earth as a man—in human form, such as we are. The things He did on the earth were done in a human body, under the power and anointing of the Holy Ghost.

When Jesus raised the dead back to life, healed the sick and diseased, opened the eyes of the blind, rebuked and cast out demons, resisted the devil's temptations, He did it all through faith in the power and authority of God, and by the anointing of the Holy Ghost. This same faith and anointing are available to us today.

As Jesus did, we can and should resist the devil, not giving in to the temptation to sin. We have been given the ability through faith to lay hands on the sick so that they may be made whole. We also have authority over demons, through the name of Jesus, therefore, we can command them to flee, and they must flee. The Holy Ghost is our Helper and is always with us, for the benefit of all those who desire to live righteously. The Lord will always make it possible to achieve holiness.

God is saying, "you must be holy, for I am holy."

HOW IS GOD HOLY?

God is unlike other gods, who are made of wood and metal, and crafted by man according to his own imaginations. Man has a visual image in his head of how he wants his god to look, then builds it according to these mental blueprints. In this, the man displays power and control over his god — through the works of his own hands. He will either make his god in his own image, or in the likeness of some other creature, real or imagined.

God has no beginning or end. Therefore, He is not a created being. He certainly was not crafted or designed by any work of man. God is a Spirit *(John 4:24)*; therefore, He has no physical form that can be seen by natural man, which makes it impossible for Him to be duplicated. God, being Spirit, is not limited to one physical location, unlike gods made of stone. Because He is a Spirit, He inhabits all time and space. With the Lord, one day is like a thousand years, and a thousand years like one day *(2 Peter 3:8)*.

Because idols are made of earthly material, they will eventually wear or rust out. For this reason they require regular repair and maintenance. God, who is self-existent (Jehovah), requires no such maintenance. Nor will He rust or wear away. God has always existed, and will continue to be. When God told Moses to go to Pharaoh and command him to "let my people go," Moses asked God, "and whom shall I say sent me?" God said, "I Am Who I Am." In other words,

> GOD SAID, "I AM WHO I AM."

God is who He is, and will be who He wants to be.

God, through His holy power, is able to meet all the needs of His people. He provides salvation, assistance, guidance, rebuke, correction, healing, and protection. Man-made gods have no power; God is All-Powerful. Idols were created by man; God is the Creator and Sustainer of life, and the universe.

There is no sin found in God. Unlike man, He cannot lie. He loves unconditionally, and forgives freely. He harbors no bitterness in His heart, and holds no grudges. God keeps His promises. He will never fail.

God is the All-Seeing, All-Knowing One. Idols have eyes, but they cannot see. They have ears, but they cannot hear. A mouth, but they cannot speak. When we cry out to God from a pure heart, He hears us and answers our prayers according to His will. He strengthens us when we are weak. His grace is sufficient for all of our needs.

The Hebrew word for holy (qadash) means: sacred, to be (make, pronounce) clean.

When God spoke to Moses out of a burning bush on Mount Horeb (a.k.a. Sinai), God instructed Moses to not come any closer, and to remove his sandals from his feet because the place where Moses stood was holy ground.

Sandals were the common form of foot covering in biblical times. They were used for decoration as well as protection. Footwear was removed indoors, in sacred areas, and during mourning. (HarperCollins Bible Dictionary)

God appeared to Moses in a flame of fire out of

the midst of a bush, therefore, that space was made consecrated: a sacred place. Accordingly, God told Moses to remove his sandals. Wherever God's presence appears, by virtue of His presence, the place is made holy.

This is why God requires you and I to be holy. Our bodies, being the temple where God's Spirit dwells, are made clean by virtue of God's presence. Therefore, we must keep our temples clean, and unspotted from sin. Sin should not be found in our members. Sin is like a pollutant; it contaminates. Because God is a holy God, it is impossible for Him to dwell in the midst of sin. Holiness and unholiness cannot co-exist in the same space.

UNHOLINESS CANNOT INHERIT THE KINGDOM

Why else must we be holy? Because an unholy people cannot inherit the kingdom of God.

God promised Israel a land of their own (Canaan).

The Bible calls Canaan God's habitation on the earth *(Exodus 15:17)*. It's a place where God would dwell among Israel and be their God, and they would be His people. Canaan was God's holy place on earth. Israel was prevented from entering Canaan for 40 years. Why? Because they were unholy, disobedient, and a stiff-necked people *(Exodus 32:9)*. Their disobedience precluded their immediate entry into Canaan.

So, we see that if God would not allow Israel to enter Canaan—His earthly habitation—being unclean, then how much more should we expect to enter heaven—God's habitation for eternity—being unclean? God will never allow anything corrupt to enter heaven, thereby defiling it. In order to inherit God's holy kingdom we must be, and remain, holy.

It's natural for us to want to rest exclusively on what Jesus' blood did for us on the cross, the assumption being that since Jesus paid the ultimate price for our sins, there's nothing more for us to do—wrong! We do have a role to play in our continued salvation. God expects us to remain unspotted from the world *(James*

1:27). We are not to go back and wallow in the mud (as a sow, after she is clean) once we have been sanctified by the blood of Jesus. And although God's grace offers forgiveness should we re-offend, His grace is not given for us to continue in sin. We abuse His grace when we continue practicing sin. God forbid, may it never be *(Romans 6:1-2)*.

HOLINESS IS THE LIFE OF A SPIRIT-FILLED BELIEVER

Holiness is clean, sacred living (physically, mentally, and spiritually). Holiness carries over into every area of our lives: in our relationship with God, in our relationships and interactions with people, in our marriage, in our thoughts, words, deeds, and in how we possess our bodies; all of it must be kept holy.

The Spirit of God dwells in all Spirit-filled believers, therefore, we are the temple of God. The Bible tells us not to destroy this temple with sin, but to keep it holy, or

God will destroy us *(1 Corinthians 3:16-17)*. Sin destroys the body, and impure thoughts destroy the mind; these thoughts eventually work their way into the heart. Therefore, keeping our thoughts pure also helps to keep our hearts pure.

We can control our thoughts by constantly renewing our mind in the word. Think on pure and holy things, while rebuking evil thoughts. When unholy thoughts present themselves to you, don't dwell on them, or embrace them, but push them far away as often as they pop up. If you begin to dwell on these thoughts, the longer you dwell on them, they begin to consume your mind, competing with and eventually pushing out the clean, holy thoughts of God. If you want to be holy in mind and thought, learn to keep God foremost in your heart, and seek to control your impure thoughts.

> A DEFILED TEMPLE IS AN UNHOLY TEMPLE.

A defiled temple is an unholy temple. It amazes me the amount of people who profess to be Christians while embracing a lifestyle of sin. They have not learned to walk upright in righteousness, remaining chaste before God. Like Israel, they have found another lover and have not kept themselves only to God.

After God delivered Israel physically from Egyptian bondage, they were still not yet mentally devoted to Him, and went whoring after other gods. Their desire to continue their relationship with these gods far outweighed their desire to devote themselves wholeheartedly to the one true God. They defiled themselves by serving idols. Holiness requires that we remain exclusive to God. We cannot serve two gods; for we will either love the one, and hate the other.

Just like God's capacity to love is great, so is His capacity to feel hurt at the rejection of man also great. God told the Prophet Jeremiah: *I've loved Israel. I made them my people and I became their God. Yet, Israel has not remained faithful to me. She has desired other gods more than me. Every time I turn around, Israel goes whoring after other gods.*

This rejection by Israel hurt God tremendously. He wants to have an exclusive relationship with us, where there is loving devotion one for the other. God has no interest in sharing us with another. Once we make the decision to serve Him, we must then remain faithful to Him, no longer the servants of sin.

How do we remain faithful to God? In the same way we are faithful to our spouse: by being committed to and honoring our marriage vows, not seeking to disavow ourselves from our spouse; by not allowing our hearts to become attached to someone other than our spouse; and by being honest, trustworthy, and faithful to our spouse. We should not allow anyone, or anything, to interfere with our marriage, or place a wedge between us and our spouse.

In a similar way, our faithfulness to God keeps us chaste in our relationship with Him. We do not seek to disavow ourselves from Him, or go back on our commitment to Him, or sin against Him by serving other gods. Our faithfulness to God also compels us to be obedient to Him, and to honor His word. We should not place anyone, or anything, above our relationship with God, or allow our hearts to become emotionally attached to anyone or anything else besides Him. God should be, and remain, first and foremost in our lives. And we should be committed to living our lives in unwavering devotion to Him.

GOD WILL SANCTIFY HIS PEOPLE

"Thou in thy mercy hast led forth the people which thou hast redeemed: thou has guided them in thy strength unto thy holy habitation" *(Exodus 15:13)*. Israel is a typology of the church. Similar to how God redeemed Israel from bondage and led them to His holy (earthly) habitation, by way of the wilderness, He has also redeemed the church through the blood of Jesus Christ, and is leading us into His holy (heavenly) habitation, by way of the wilderness. Not all of those who were redeemed from Egypt made it to the promised land; some of them died in the wilderness, because of disobedience and sin.

Unfortunately, not all of the church will make it to heaven. Sadly, some will, like Israel, die along the way because of disobedience and sin. Some Christians still find pleasure in sin, and simply refuse to give it up. These have not yet learned how to crucify the works of the flesh, and to be led by the Spirit. The Holy Ghost leads us into all truth. But if we refuse to obey and follow after the leading of the Holy Ghost, preferring instead to follow our own path, we will no doubt end up like those who died in the wilderness: hopelessly lost.

God has prepared for His children a home in heaven. To inherit this home, we must be sanctified (set apart, separate from the world). Before Israel could enter into Canaan, God needed to sanctify them, and make them holy. God is also sanctifying us in preparation of our ascent into heaven.

In Exodus 19:10, God told Moses, *Sanctify the people in preparation of my descent before the people on Mount Sinai.* Israel went through two days of preparation to meet the Lord on Mount Sinai. God commanded them to wash their clothes, to wash themselves, and to not have intimate relations with their spouse. Israel needed to be clean before God's glory descended before them on Mount Sinai.

Aaron and his sons (the priests) had to wear special garments (holy garments) when they ministered before the Lord. These garments set them apart as holy unto the Lord *(Exodus 28:35-36)*. They had to be thoroughly washed and cleaned before they could robe themselves in these garments. The garments were for glory and beauty. Nothing corrupt or unclean could stand before the Lord God.

Are you fully prepared to stand before God in all His glory? Have you been thoroughly washed and cleaned by the Holy Ghost in preparation for your heavenly meeting with God? Allow the Holy Ghost to sanctify you, for there is no other way to see our Saviour's face in peace.

Chapter 8

HOLINESS 101

SOUND DOCTRINE

Every Christian has an obligation to guard and protect the sacred truths of the gospel, and to reject false doctrine, which leads us astray and away from the truth. God has entrusted us with His holy word, and it is up to us to guard the sacred truths found in it. These truths provide a foundation for the Christian faith, lead us into a deeper revelation of God, and provide correction when we begin to stray from it.

Having a thorough understanding of the word, and a reverence for it, should help guard us against an infiltration of false doctrine, which can be detrimental to the believer.

Being firmly rooted and grounded in the word is the foundation every believer needs to lead a holy life. Sound doctrine is the foundation of holiness. Without a firm foundation, it is easy to be deceived, and tossed to-and-fro with every wind of doctrine which deceptively masquerades itself as truth.

We need to mature into holiness, no longer babes who are easily tempted to sin against God. Holiness, therefore, requires a maturation process. It doesn't happen overnight. When we are born-again, our souls are saved but our flesh is not. We are still housed in the same earthly bodies; and our flesh will always be tempted to sin, for that is its nature. Therefore, we must learn to crucify the flesh daily, working diligently every day toward meeting God's ideal standards of godliness.

Holiness is not an option. It is something God not only expects, but absolutely requires from us. Being firmly rooted and grounded in sound doctrine starts us on the right path to living according to God's holy standards.

NOT JUST A SUNDAY MORNING THING

Salvation is not something we do on Sunday, then take a break from it the rest of the week to pursue the fulfillment of our own worldly lusts. Neither is holiness just a Sunday morning thing.

Holiness requires a devotion to God. It's having our minds and hearts committed to living within the boundaries of the laws God has put in place for the purpose of bringing us closer to Him. Again, in order to inherit the kingdom of God, we must be holy.

Israel rejected God's laws when they decided to build a golden calf in the wilderness to worship as a substitute for God. In this, they willfully sinned against

God. God explicitly commanded them not to worship any other gods besides Him. He is the one true God who delivered them from Egyptian bondage to lead them into a land He had prepared especially for them.

When we decide to take a break from God, it leads us out of His will, into the danger zone, and away from the safety of God's protection and covering, which leaves us naked and exposed. We take a chance every time we step outside of His will, because there is no guarantee we'll ever make it back in in time. So why even take that chance? Matthew 24:13 says, "he that endures to the end shall be saved." We must run this Christian race with perseverance and endurance. We have to be committed to seeing it through to the end.

Holiness is a Godly-lifestyle which must be fully embraced by all believers in order to reach the pinnacle of salvation. This is God's highest standard for man on earth.

The Bible teaches us that when the *Day of the Lord* comes, there will be new heavens and a new earth. The old heavens and earth will be destroyed, along with sin and all its evil works. Only righteousness will dwell in the new heavens and the new earth *(2 Peter 3:10-13).*

This shows us how much God hates sin. And while sin can still be found on the earth today, it will not, however, be allowed to continue its destructive force forever; for God will soon destroy it once and for all, along with the earth. He will then create a new earth, which will finally bring the earth back to its original sin-free state, which is more in line with God's principles and values.

Therefore, as Christians we need to be mindful of the things we embrace while we are housed in our temporary earthly bodies. This earth and all its worldly-goods are not our inheritance. Our inheritance is eternal in the heavens, where moth and rust cannot contaminate. We should not embrace sin. We should, however, embrace godliness. Sin is destructive and only leads to eternal separation from God. God's nature is holy; we must also be holy.

NO PHARISEES ALLOWED

Jesus had many notable encounters with the Pharisees, and warned His disciples to not be like them. While the Pharisees were devout Jews and steeped in Jewish tradition, they did not serve God with their hearts. Jesus told His disciples to follow what they say, but not to do what they do.

The Pharisees were teachers and leaders among the Jews. Jesus criticized them for being religious outwardly but full of hypocrisy within. They prayed long prayers to be seen of men. And when they wore the traditional Jewish garments and implements, theirs were even more garish and attention-grabbing than others, giving them the appearance before men of being more spiritual than most. But Jesus said that God saw their hearts and knew that the things they did were just for show, and were not done with sincerity and devotion to God.

Our service and devotion to God should not just be lip-service. Our actions should always line up with our words, and we should serve God out of a pure heart, not full of hypocrisy and showy displays of devotion.

Unlike the Pharisees, we should seek to please God,

rather than man. Our devotion to God should lead us into a more intimate relationship with Him. And as we get closer to God and He in turn begins to reveal more of Himself to us, we should then begin to become a reflection of Him, taking on more of His characteristics. His revelation of Himself to us is supposed to be for us to look into the light of His countenance and reflect back to Him what we see in Him.

Moses, who spent a lot of time in the mountain with God, began to reflect the very image of God on his own countenance, so much so that whenever Moses came down from the mountain, his face shone. People were able to look upon his face and see a revelation of God. Moses reflected upon his own face an image of God's glory. People saw him and knew that he had spent time in the presence of God.

Holiness is a reflection of God's glory. When people see us walking in holiness, it should be for them a revelation of the very image of God's holiness.

LOVE NOT THE WORLD

The world is deceitfully wicked. Deceitful, because it comes wrapped in a bow with pretty packaging, and handed to you like a present on a silver platter. It's not until you unwrap the bow, and tear into the packaging, that you really see what's inside: the lust of the flesh, the lust of the eye, and the pride of life.

The Bible tells us not to love the world, neither the things that are in the world; because whoever loves the world, the love of the Father is not in him. He that is a friend of the world is not a friend of God. It's impossible to love the world while professing our love for God.

The world's philosophies and ways of thinking are the complete opposites of God's. In the world, anything goes. If it makes you feel good, then you should indulge, engage, and submit. The world teaches that you shouldn't deny yourself any desires or pleasures. Not only should you enjoy them, but you should enjoy them in excess. Nothing is off-limits, if it makes you feel good.

This is *not* what Scripture teaches us. It shows us the true nature of our flesh: sinful, wicked, ungodly, and unholy. For this reason, the Bible tells us to crucify the flesh daily. It implores us not to walk after the flesh, but to walk after the Spirit. When we walk after the flesh, it will always lead us away from God, in the pursuit of worldly lusts and pleasures. These pursuits are always outside of the will of God. The world and all its lusts will one day pass away. But the one who does the will of God will live forever *(1 John 2:17)*.

In order to live forever with God we must completely sever our relationship with the world. We must cut all ungodly ties and walk according to the leading of the Spirit. The Spirit will only lead us in the direction that is pleasing, and acceptable to God. When we walk after the Spirit, and not after the flesh, the Spirit will lead us into godliness.

L.O.V.E. - LOVE

There is an epidemic sweeping the land: mean, vengeful Christians. You see them everywhere. Angry Christians at the mall, on the job, even in church. And they are often the loudest, most visible Christians the world sees. Because they are often more visible, this is the unfortunate image the world applies to all Christians, which gives the world a negative image of Christianity, and ultimately of God. This epidemic needs to stop. It's time we put an end to it once and for all. We are God's representatives on earth. But how can we say we represent God when we're not walking in love?

He that says he loves God, but hates his brother, is a liar. If we truly have the love of God within us, it will compel us to love our fellow man. Without love, we have nothing.

Love is the greatest force in the world. Love can combat evil. Love can even melt the most hardened man, bringing him to tears. There's nothing greater than love. God is love; and He showed His great love for us in that while we were yet sinners, Christ died for the ungodly. "For God so loved the world, that he gave his only begotten Son, that whosoever believeth in him should not perish, but have everlasting life" *(John 3:16)*. Love compels us to give of ourselves sacrificially so that others might live.

Love is a manifestation of true holiness. What's on the inside will eventually manifest itself outwardly. If God's Spirit truly lives in us, it will show itself visually, outwardly. When we're walking in love, the world will be able to look at us and see that there's something different about us. Our old sinful nature has been removed, and we have been made into new creatures in Christ Jesus. Therefore, we no longer cling to feelings and emotions of the past. It's okay to release hate, bitterness, envy, etc., and allow God to make us over. Release it so that you are free to walk in pure love.

MUST JESUS BEAR THE CROSS ALONE?

We often hear about Christ's sufferings, but we don't like to talk much about our own. We'll talk candidly about the unimaginable abuse and pain Jesus endured at the hands of evil men: the beatings, the torture, the lies, the persecution, the nail scarred hands and feet, the sword plunged deep into His side, the crown of thorns placed on His head in humiliation—the inexcusable brutality and suffering endured by an innocent man. We'll even acknowledge that yes, He did it all for me. Jesus died for my sins; it should have been me on that cross, but praise God He took my place. We'll acknowledge *His* suffering, but *we* don't want to suffer. No one wants to suffer.

As was stated before, godliness and persecution often go hand-in-hand. If we want to reign with Christ, we must also suffer with Him. Must Jesus bear the cross alone? Is Christ the only one who is to suffer for the sake of the gospel? Should we only inherit all of the good treasures of the kingdom, but not endure the sufferings that often go along with the inheritance?

The early church was persecuted, imprisoned, and even brutally killed—all because they were followers of Christ, whom the world did not believe was the Messiah. These people walked with Jesus, were taught by Him, saw the persecutions He endured at the hands of wicked men. They also saw His grace and strength under the persecution, and that no matter how hard they persecuted Him, Jesus never lost focus, and never sinned against God. He came to earth on a mission, and He was determined to see that mission through to the end.

Jesus Christ is the rock, the cornerstone, of our Christian faith. It is His life and mission that we should emulate. His time spent on earth, however brief, was plagued with tests and trials, temptations, and suffering. His was not an easy life, nor has He promised one to us. In fact, He warned us of the fiery trials to come. But we are commissioned to endure hardness as a good soldier, for it is the testing of our faith that works patient endurance. If we indeed are willing to suffer with Him, we shall also reign with Him.

קְדוּשָׁה
HOLINESS

Chapter 9

ISRAEL'S TRAINING IN HOLINESS

The grooming of Israel began immediately when God brought them out of Egypt. God used Moses to teach Israel His commandments and ordinances. God no longer saw Israel as slaves, for He had delivered them from their bondage and set them free. This freedom granted them a new identity - as the chosen and beloved of God. God intended to erase the stain that 430 years of captivity had heaped upon them. But it quickly became evident that this would not be an easy task.

During their time in Egypt, Israel was exposed to an enormous amount of sin and wickedness. They habitually practiced heathen rituals, and worshiped and served pagan gods. It was clearly evident that these heathen practices had become deeply woven into the fabric of their daily lives.

Israel's lack of knowledge in the God of their fathers — Abraham, Isaac, and Jacob — led them to worship other gods who were once foreign to them, causing them to become corrupt. Because of this corruption, God needed to purify them before they could enter the promised land. This purification took place during the 40 years they were made to wander in the wilderness. During these wanderings, Moses taught them about the God of their fathers, and encouraged them to obey all of His laws.

God granted Moses unprecedented access into His presence in order to transfer His laws to Moses for Israel's instruction. These instructions were specifically designed to aide in Israel's transformation, as a holy nation.

> "And the Lord spake unto Moses, saying,
> Speak unto all the congregation of the children of Israel,
> and say unto them, Ye shall be holy:
> for I the Lord your God am holy"
> (Leviticus 19:1-2).

> "For I am the Lord
> that bringeth you up out of the land of Egypt,
> to be your God:
> ye shall therefore be holy, for I am holy"
> (Leviticus 11:45).

God wanted to make certain that Israel understood what He expected of them—holiness. They were not to be like other nations; they were to be different. Because of this, God required Israel to put away their heathen rituals, their idols, and to serve Him only. They were to be a light to the nations around them; and this light was to reflect the light and the holiness of God, who is more powerful than all other gods.

God set boundaries and limitations for Israel, which are clearly stated in His commandments and ordinances—a portion of which can be found in Deuteronomy 5:

> 1 And Moses called all Israel, and said unto them, Hear, O Israel, the statutes and judgments which I speak in your ears this day, that ye may learn them, and keep, and do them.
> 2 The Lord our God made a covenant with us in Horeb.
> 3 The Lord made not this covenant with our fathers, but with us, even us, who are all of us here alive this day.
> 4 The Lord talked with you face to face in the mount out of the midst of the fire,
> 5 (I stood between the Lord and you at

that time, to shew you the word of the Lord: for ye were afraid by reason of the fire, and went not up into the mount;) saying,

6 I am the Lord thy God, which brought thee out of the land of Egypt, from the house of bondage.

7 Thou shalt have none other gods before me.

8 Thou shalt not make thee any graven image, or any likeness of any thing that is in heaven above, or that is in the earth beneath, or that is in the waters beneath the earth:

9 Thou shalt not bow down thyself unto them, nor serve them: for I the Lord thy God am a jealous God, visiting the iniquity of the fathers upon the children unto the third and fourth generation of them that hate me,

10 And shewing mercy unto thousands

of them that love me and keep my commandments.

11 Thou shalt not take the name of the Lord thy God in vain: for the Lord will not hold him guiltless that taketh his name in vain.

12 Keep the sabbath day to sanctify it, as the Lord thy God hath commanded thee.

13 Six days thou shalt labour, and do all thy work:

14 But the seventh day is the sabbath of the Lord thy God: in it thou shalt not do any work, thou, nor thy son, nor thy daughter, nor thy manservant, nor thy maidservant, nor thine ox, nor thine ass, nor any of thy cattle, nor thy stranger that is within thy gates; that thy manservant and thy maidservant may rest as well as thou.

15 And remember that thou wast a servant in the land of Egypt, and that

the Lord thy God brought thee out thence through a mighty hand and by a stretched out arm: therefore the Lord thy God commanded thee to keep the sabbath day.

16 Honour thy father and thy mother, as the Lord thy God hath commanded thee; that thy days may be prolonged, and that it may go well with thee, in the land which the Lord thy God giveth thee.

17 Thou shalt not kill.

18 Neither shalt thou commit adultery.

19 Neither shalt thou steal.

20 Neither shalt thou bear false witness against thy neighbour.

21 Neither shalt thou desire thy neighbour's wife, neither shalt thou covet thy neighbour's house, his field, or his manservant, or his maidservant, his ox, or his ass, or any thing that is thy neighbour's.

As we can clearly see here, God had high expectations for Israel. In all, God gave them a total of 613 Commandments. Some of these were "positive commandments," which they were to adhere to, and some were "negative commandments," which they were to abstain from. All of these helped to make a clear distinction between them and the other nations around them, who lived according to their own prescribed standards. As God's people, Israel was now expected to live according to His standards, which were designed to make them holy.

קְדוּשָׁה
HOLINESS

Chapter 10

ISRAEL'S DIETARY RESTRICTIONS

As we just saw, the laws God gave to Moses were designed to differentiate Israel from other nations, and to make them holy. Included in these laws are *dietary laws*, which Moses records in two sections of the Torah: Leviticus 11 and Deuteronomy 14.

DIETARY LAWS

In his book: *"Jewish Culture & Customs. A Sampler Of Jewish Life,"* Steve Herzig says, the rules concerning the eating of animals, birds, fish, and insects form the major portion of these dietary laws. A *kosher* (fit or proper) animal must meet two requirements: It must chew its cud and have completely split hooves forming two toes. Kosher fish are required to have fins and scales. Certain fowl — such as ostrich, raven, stork, owl, pelican, and eagle — are not fit for consumption. Three kinds of insects — locusts, crickets, and grasshoppers — are permitted to be eaten. None of these creatures can be eaten unless slaughtered specifically for consumption.

Herzig goes on to say, there is a method in Jewish custom for killing animals for food. A *shoket* (ritual slaughterer) must do the killing, thus eliminating the sport of hunting for those observant Jews. A *shoket* places a *chalif* (specific knife) across the throat of the animal. With one swift cut, the trachea and esophagus are severed. This procedure is regarded as the most humane for the animal and is the best way to drain the blood. The Bible does not allow consumption of fat or blood *(Leviticus 3:17)*. Accordingly, *kosher* meat must be salted for at least 30 minutes to drain any remaining blood. If this is not done, the rabbis deem the meat to be *traif* (unclean).

God gave food to mankind for nourishment and sustenance; and it is to be received with thanksgiving. I also believe God wants us to find enjoyment in food.

In every culture (not just Jewish culture), food is often shared with others during certain events, holidays, and special occasions. Food is to be celebrated, and not wasted. It should never become a stumbling block or an occasion for offense, but thoroughly enjoyed by all for its ability to bring people together, and its ability to nourish. Food, of course, should never be sacrificed to idols—as was the custom with certain pagan rituals in biblical Israel, and is still the custom for some today. Following God's dietary laws will no doubt make one healthy and well.

These food laws that God gave to Israel set them apart from other nations, who through their rebellion, used food in ways other than what God intended: such as in sacrifice to idols.

NOURISHMENT

According to *"The HarperCollins Bible Dictionary,"* bread was the chief staple food in biblical times. The most common grains were barley, wheat, and emmer (hulled wheat), from which bread was baked.

Next to bread, were fruits, vegetables, and dairy products (which derived more from goats than cows) in the form of cheese, curds, and butters.

Common fruits were grapes (used mostly in the form of oil), figs, dates, apples, and pomegranates.

Vegetables consisted of beans, cucumbers, lentils, onions, leeks, and garlic.

Animals, both domesticated and wild, such as deer, gazelle, fish, and fowl were also consumed. Boiling and roasting were the preferred means of preparing meat. The blood had to be drained, since God instructed them that they were not to consume blood, as the life was contained in the blood *(Genesis 9:4-6).* Unclean animals were not to be consumed (*Leviticus 11*).

Their diet was rounded out by spices and other natural products such as salt and honey.

SOCIAL CONNECTION TO FOOD

Food also connects people socially. Weddings, feasts, and Jewish holidays were often celebrated with food. According to Herzig, "Marriage is regarded as one of the most important and significant decisions in the lives of Jewish people. The Torah clearly states that God made 'an help fit' for Adam because 'it is not good that the man should be alone'" (*Genesis 2:18*).

Marriage is seen as God's divine plan for mankind. When a man and woman marry, it is a time of great joy and celebration. Herzig says, today it is still a Jewish custom on the Sabbath before the wedding for the groom to go up to the platform to read the Torah. The congregation showers him with candies, representing wishes for a sweet married life.

In biblical Israel, weddings were usually festive

occasions complete with singing, dancing, and feasting that lasted one or two weeks. Jesus attended a wedding feast in Cana of Galilee, where he turned water into the best quality wine, to the surprise of the governor in charge of the wedding festivities *(John 2)*.

Again, food is to be enjoyed for its nourishment capabilities as well as its ability to unite people socially. It is when we abuse or misuse it that we run into problems. Since the beginning of time, mankind has always found ways to change the natural use of things (such as food) away from God's original intent, into something immoral and sacrilegious, thereby corrupting their souls, and dishonoring God.

God, intending to eradicate the unholy and ungodly moral habits Israel acquired while in Egypt, gave them these dietary restrictions to follow. These laws would certainly help to distinguish Israel from other nations, who were still engaging in these harmful practices.

IN THE BEGINNING

The following is an excerpt from Genesis 2:

⁹ And out of the ground made the Lord God to grow every tree that is pleasant to the sight, and good for food; the tree of life also in the midst of the garden, and the tree of knowledge of good and evil.

¹⁶ And the Lord God commanded the man, saying, Of every tree of the garden thou mayest freely eat: ¹⁷ but of the tree of the knowledge of good and evil, thou shalt not eat of it: for in the day that thou eatest thereof thou shalt surely die.

¹⁸ And the Lord God said, It is not good that the man should be alone; I will make him an help meet for him. ¹⁹ And out of the ground the Lord God formed every beast of the field, and every fowl of the air; and brought them unto Adam to see what he would call them: and whatsoever Adam called every living creature, that was the name thereof.

[20] And Adam gave names to all cattle, and to the fowl of the air, and to every beast of the field; but for Adam there was not found an help meet for him. [21] And the Lord God caused a deep sleep to fall upon Adam, and he slept: and he took one of his ribs, and closed up the flesh instead thereof; [22] and the rib, which the Lord God had taken from man, made he a woman, and brought her unto the man. [23] And Adam said, This is now bone of my bones, and flesh of my flesh: she shall be called Woman, because she was taken out of Man.

It is quite possible that God originally created the animals to be a companion of sorts for man (not in place of the woman, but as "furry" companions, if you will). When God said it is not good for man to be alone, the first thing He did was form the animals out of the ground and brought them to Adam to name *(see Genesis 2:18-19, above)*. But after the disobedience and subsequent fall of man, the dynamics of this relationship between man and animal may have changed, causing man to develop a lust for meat, no longer seeing them as companions, but now as a food source. This change may have created a need for God to distinguish for man which animals were suitable for consumption, and which were not.

God told Adam that he was free to eat from every tree of the garden, except the *tree of the knowledge of good and evil (Genesis 2:16-17)*. So, it stands to reason that God's original intent for man was for him to be a vegetarian, not a carnivore (meat-eater).

The Bible says, everything God made was good: the earth, the ground, man, the animals. But once the serpent beguiled the woman, causing her to eat from the *tree of the knowledge of good and evil,* God pronounced a curse on the serpent calling him "cursed above all cattle, and above every beast of the field" *(Genesis 3:14)*. The curse also relegated him to crawling upon his belly and eating the dust of the ground the rest of his days.

God also cursed the ground, saying it shall thus

bring forth thorns and thistles and that man shall eat the plants of the field — which were now cursed. Prior to this, man had eaten the sweet fruit of the trees. But God said, because of man's disobedience, he would now eat of the bitterness of the field *(Genesis 3:17-18)*.

EFFECTS OF THE CURSE

After being banished from the garden, Adam intimately knew his wife, Eve, and she conceived two sons: Cain and Abel. Cain — the elder brother — was a farmer (a tiller of the ground), and Abel kept his family's sheep.

Over the course of time, the hard labor put forth by man yielded a harvest. Both Cain and Abel brought an offering from the harvest unto the Lord. Cain's offering came from the fruit of the ground (which was now cursed). This could possibly explain why his offering was not accepted by God, and Abel's was. Abel, on the other hand, brought an offering of the firstlings of his flock. God had more respect for Abel's offering than Cain's *(Genesis 4:4-5)*. Cain's anger and resentment eventually led him to kill his brother, Abel.

Because of the curse, man now has to labor for his food; whereas before, God had freely given it to him. But now by the sweat of his brow shall man eat his food *(Genesis 3:19)*. The term *hunters and gatherers* came about because of the way people hunted animals and gathered wild plants for their food prior to the advent of farming.

Today, we are still living under the curse. We still have to work for our food by the sweat of our brow. Sometimes the ground releases its harvest abundantly, and sometimes it does not. But thankfully today, because of modern technology, the process has become a bit more streamlined and we are able to process more of our food with machinery, reducing the amount of manpower that was once required. And we are also able to process a bigger quantity, faster, shortening the amount of time it takes to get the produce to market, and eventually to the home table.

But the ground is still cursed. It still brings forth thorns and thistles. And there are times when it fails to produce a harvest. And, the serpent is still cursed above every creature, and still crawls on its belly eating the dust of the ground. But soon, God will release the earth from its curse. And what a glorious day that will be!

קְדוּשָׁה
HOLINESS

Chapter 11

ISRAEL'S SACRIFICE

In the Old Testament, sacrifices were offered to God in worship. They expressed repentance from sin and obedience to God. The Lord gave very detailed instructions to Moses on how these sacrifices were to be conducted, which Moses records in two books of the Torah: Leviticus and Numbers.

These sacrificial offerings consisted of: sin and

trespass (guilt) offerings, burnt offerings, grain (meal) offerings, and peace offerings.

All animals sacrificed to God were to come from among the herd (cattle) or flock. Only domestic animals could be sacrificed. All were to be unblemished; that is, they could not be diseased or deformed in any way.

Grain offerings, given to God in thankfulness, were required to have oil and frankincense added. The grain could be offered in its natural state, baked in an oven, made on the griddle, or prepared in a pan. No grain was to be presented to the Lord with leaven or any sweetener, such as honey. Every grain offering was seasoned with salt. Nothing plain or bland was to be offered to the Lord.

Everything sacrificed on the altar, be it animal, bird, or grain, was an offering made by fire. The fire purified the offering, and the smoke from the sacrifice was a soothing aroma to the Lord.

BURNT OFFERING

The *burnt offering* was probably the most common of all the offerings. It was a free-will offering of a male from the *herd,* without blemish. The person making the sacrifice laid his hand on the head of the animal—making it acceptable for him to make an atonement on his behalf—and killed it. The priest then offered up the blood, and sprinkled the blood around on the altar. The animal was then skinned and cut into pieces, with the pieces, the head, and the fat placed on the altar. The animal's entrails (internal parts) and legs were then washed with water to remove any excrement and, thus, making it clean, prior to being placed on the altar.

The smoke from the burnt offering rose up to God as a soothing aroma. It was a sacrifice made voluntarily and obediently to God. The fire provided purification, and the water a cleansing.

A burnt offering from the *flock* was either a sheep or a goat; also a male without blemish. The offering from the flock was conducted in the same manner as the offering from the herd: the person laid his hand on the animal's head, killed it, and the priest sprinkled its blood around on the altar. The cut-up pieces, its head, and fat were placed on the altar, with its entrails (internal parts) and legs having been washed with water.

If one chose to bring a burnt offering of *birds* it had to be either a turtledove, or young pigeon. The bird's head was wrung off and placed on the altar. The blood was drained on the side of the altar. Its feathers were plucked, and the priest tore it by its wings, but did not sever it, then offered the bird up in smoke on the altar by fire unto the Lord.

GRAIN (MEAL) OFFERING

God instructed Moses to prepare the *grain offering* in the following manner: The grain should be of fine flour. Oil and frankincense (when burnt emits a fragrant aroma) were poured on the fine flour. The priest then took a handful of the mixture and offered it in smoke on the altar. The remaining grain belonged to the priest.

PEACE OFFERING

The *peace offering* was symbolic of peace and fellowship between the worshiper and God. This offering came from among the herd (probably a bull or cow), or the flock (a lamb or goat). The *peace offering* could be either *male* or *female*, but without any blemish. The process for the peace offering was similar to that of the burnt offering: the one presenting the sacrifice laid his hand on the animal's head, and killed it. The priest then sprinkled the animal's blood around on the altar.

SIN OFFERING

Sin offerings were to make restitution for anyone who sinned *unintentionally* by committing any of the things the Lord had commanded not to be done. The offerings were slightly different depending on whether the offender was a priest, a leader, a lay person, or the whole congregation.

If the *anointed priest* sinned so as to bring guilt on the people, his sin offering was to be made for his sins in the following manner:

- A bull, without blemish.
- The person (in this case, the priest that sinned) laid his hand on the animal's head, and killed it.
- The anointed priest dipped his finger in the blood seven times and sprinkled the blood before the Lord, in front of the veil of the sanctuary.
- The priest placed some of the blood on the horns of the altar of the fragrant incense.
- All remaining blood was poured out at the base of the altar.
- The fat, and the two kidneys with fat on them, were laid on the altar.
- The bull's hide, flesh, head, legs, and entrails were taken outside the camp and burned.

If the *whole congregation* sinned, the sin offering was to be made as follows:

- A bull, without blemish.

- The elders laid hands on the animal's head and killed it for the congregation.
- The anointed priest dipped his finger in the blood seven times and sprinkled the blood before the Lord, in front of the veil of the sanctuary.
- The priest placed some of the blood on the horns of the altar of the fragrant incense.
- All remaining blood was poured out at the base of the altar.
- The fat, and the two kidneys with fat on them, were laid on the altar.
- The bull's hide, flesh, head, legs, and entrails were taken outside the camp and burned.

If a *leader* sinned, his sin offering was made in the following way:

- A goat, male without blemish.
- The leader who sinned laid his hand on the animal's head, and killed it.
- The priest dipped his finger in the blood and put it on the horns of the altar, pouring the remaining

blood out at the base of the altar.
- The fat was offered in smoke on the altar, similar to the fat of the sacrifice of peace offering.

If a *lay person* sinned, the atonement for his sins were as follows:
- A goat or lamb, female without blemish.
- The lay person laid his hand on the animal's head, and killed it.
- The priest dipped his finger in the blood and put it on the horns of the altar, pouring the remaining blood out at the base of the altar.
- The fat was offered in smoke on the altar, similar to the fat of the sacrifice of peace offering.

TRESPASS (GUILT) OFFERING

The *trespass (guilt) offering* addressed unintentional sins with an emphasis on *sins of omission*. A person became guilty if he sinned, and was to confess his sin when it became known to him, and bring a trespass offering to the Lord to make atonement for the sins he had committed. Trespass offerings addressed sins against others.

The violations that warranted a trespass offering were: 1.) a witness who did not come forward to testify after witnessing a violation, or having firsthand knowledge, such as hearing the violator confess to the sin. 2.) a person touched any unclean thing, whether a carcass of an unclean beast, or the carcass of unclean cattle, or a carcass of unclean swarming things; or if he touched human uncleanness. 3.) a person swore thoughtlessly, i.e. rash oath making, whether for good or bad.

The guilty party was to confess his sins and bring his trespass offering to the Lord to make atonement for his sins.

- A goat or lamb, female without blemish.
- The priest shall make atonement on his behalf.

If the guilty party could not afford a lamb, then he

could bring *two turtledoves*, or *two young pigeons*, one for a sin offering and the other for a burnt offering.

- The priest first offered the sin offering, nipped its head and the front of its neck, not severing it.
- The priest sprinkled some of its blood on the side of the altar, draining the rest at the base of the altar.
- Next, the priest offered the burnt offering in the same manner as the sin offering.

If the person could not afford the two turtledoves or pigeons, he could bring the *tenth of an ephah of fine flour.*

- No oil or incense could be put on it, for it was a sin offering.
- The priest took a handful and offered it up in smoke on the altar. The remaining belonged to the priest, similar to the grain offering.

Trespass offerings were also made by someone who sinned through ignorance in the holy things of the Lord (the Lord's property), committed any of the other things forbidden by the Lord, deceived his companion, committed robbery or extortion, or found and kept something that did not belong to him. The guilty party brought an offering to the Lord, made restitution to the person who suffered the loss, with a portion going to the priest.

All of these sacrifices were just that, sacrifices. It was the Lord's way of righting a wrong that had been committed by an individual against God and/or others, thereby atoning for his sins and making him acceptable to the Lord. No sin went unpunished; but the blood of the sacrifice provided reparations for the sin, offering reconciliation between man and God.

God required Israel to bring a sacrifice for all of the sins they committed, whether intentionally or unintentionally. When the sin becomes known to the person, he first acknowledges his sin, which is the first step in the forgiveness process. When you know that you have sinned, you must first acknowledge your sin. You should also be genuinely repentant for the sin you have committed in disobeying God's laws, and be willing to make the necessary restitutions for your sin.

In Israel's case, the restitutions had been clearly established by God. Israel was to take from among the best of their herd, flock, and grain, and sacrifice it to God. This sacrifice was to be burned with fire. The animal's life was given as a substitution for the person's life, because when we sin against God a sentence of death is placed over our life. But God allowed Israel to sacrifice an animal's life in place of their own. And because the life is in the blood, the priest was required to sprinkle the animal's blood around on the altar, or place some of the blood on the horns of the altar of fragrant incense (in the case of the sin offering), thereby offering the animal's "life" as a sacrifice to God.

This is what was required of all who sinned in biblical times. Aren't you glad we don't have to do any of this today? Just imagine how often we have sinned against God, and others. We would have to slaughter a lot of animals to atone for all of our sins. (The animal-rights activists would not be happy.)

But today, Jesus has become our atoning sacrifice.

He sacrificed His life *once,* for all of our sins. His blood now covers us, making us acceptable to the Lord. This is nothing to be taken for granted. Someone had to die; and Jesus lovingly stepped up and said, *I will die for you. I will take your place on the altar of sacrifice (the cross).* He shed His blood on the cross for our sins. We owe Him our lives. As a matter of fact, our lives are no longer our own. We have been bought with a great price — the blood of Jesus Christ. His blood did what no other sacrifice could do — offer a permanent solution for sin.

The animal sacrifices offered only a temporary solution. Israel had to keep going back to the priest to offer a sacrifice each time they sinned against God. In other words, their sacrifices only provided a temporary relief from their sins. But Jesus' blood has offered a permanent solution for our sins. His blood is so potent that He only had to die once; Jesus' blood is still as effective today as it was when He first died. But this does not give us license to keep sinning. This was not the intent of Him sacrificing His life for us. Once you have been forgiven, turn completely away from sin with a truly repentant heart, and dedicate your life to serving God. Do not allow Jesus' blood to go to waste.

HOLINESS

Chapter 12

WHAT GOD EXPECTS FROM US TODAY

This Christian life that we have been called to is a consecrated life. Those whom God have called, He has also anointed. When we say yes to His call, we are saying yes to everything that goes along with it—the good as well as the bad.

Most Christians only want the blessings that come

with being in Christ. We want God to open the windows of heaven and pour out on us all of His goodness, to overflowing. We want Him to fight every battle for us, and to swoop in and rescue us from every bad situation. This highly glossed-over image of Christianity is what we readily grab hold of, almost greedily, and often with a sense of entitlement.

There, unfortunately, will be some rough roads that we must travel on the path to godliness. We may even shed a few tears. And as hard as it is for us to hear, we may also suffer heart-breaking loss. There will be persecution because persecution tends to go hand-in-hand with godliness, so be prepared. This could all potentially cause our faith to waver. But, we must have a strong conviction that even in the bad, God is still good. And He's still in control, no matter how bad the situation looks.

Our calling requires a life of sacrifice and discipline. Be prepared to sacrifice your will for God's. This is hard for some to do, as we are often strong-willed people, who always want things to go our way. But a Christian has to sacrifice his will for God's.

The desire for worldly pleasures and sin need to be put to death in our flesh. We can no longer hang onto the world's goods while seeking to inherit God's kingdom. Something has to be sacrificed for the sake of the gospel. And if we're not sacrificing earthly things, then more than likely we are sacrificing spiritual things.

Discipline is at the heart of holiness. So is obedience. Discipline, a structured and orderly process which leads to precision and self-control, is what is needed for the Christian to go from a mere believer (the initial stages of Christianity) to becoming a doer of the word, and a follower of Christ. Our actions must begin to reflect our Christian beliefs. Holiness should permeate every fiber of our being until it becomes a natural part of us — as natural as breathing. It is no longer a distant thought; it is who we are. And because this is a journey, it is who we are becoming, with the help of the Holy Ghost.

Holiness is something we must actively work at every day. When a runner trains for a marathon, he practices and prepares everyday for the big day:

stretching, working out, running several hours a day, and building up his stamina and endurance for the race. He's disciplined and focused on his goal. He sees what he wants to achieve (the finish line), and actively works toward reaching his goal day after day.

Like the runner, we must also see this as a journey: a process to be practiced every day. We are training to reach our goal — holiness — which will lead us to our final destination: heaven. God knows there will be obstacles that we must overcome in our flesh and in our minds. But the one who is focused on the prize, disciplined, and determined, will have a much better chance of achieving his goal than the one who is not.

We have an added advantage in that we have the Holy Ghost as our Helper. The Holy Ghost empowers us to live holy, helps us when we are weak, and gives us the guidance and the instructions we need to reach our goals. And if we find ourselves getting a little off course, God will assist us in getting back on course. So there is no need to fret; we are not alone in this journey. God will never leave us alone. He sends us the help we need to live holy. God wants us to live and to succeed in holiness; because holiness is God's way.

קְדוּשָׁה
HOLINESS

Chapter 13

HOLINESS TRAINING BEGINS IMMEDIATELY

Today, our introduction into holiness begins the moment we're born-again. As new believers, we are taught that we are now new creatures, and that the old godless, sinful nature has passed away, and Jesus Christ has made us brand-new. We are no longer slaves to the devil; we have been set free, delivered from the chains that once held us captive, and as such, we must now walk in the fullness of the new life we have been given through Christ.

Our course in life has been changed, and our destiny now secured. Just as God rewrote Israel's fate when He delivered them from a life of bondage, He has also rewritten our fate when He delivered us from eternal damnation and sin.

God knew what was in Israel's heart. He knew that if given the chance they would have turned around and gone back into Egypt, because, even though the life they lived in Egypt was a hard one, it was familiar to them; it was all they knew.

> **GOD KNEW WHAT WAS IN ISRAEL'S HEART.**

This new life that God expected them to embrace was unfamiliar, and unpredictable. They had to learn to trust God, which was hard for them to do. Even though they had seen His power, they still didn't know and trust Him. How could they be certain they *could* trust Him? The people they once thought they could trust — the Egyptian authorities — had stabbed them in the back, and enslaved them. So, their trust had been shaken; not to mention they had actually come to love the gods they served in Egypt. This *invisible* God was a mystery to them.

Even though Israel didn't *physically* turn back to Egypt, they did, however, turn back in their hearts when they continued to practice their heathen rituals, and continued to serve their Egyptian gods in the wilderness.

It's important for us to turn away from the old man and the life we used to live in the world. We cannot expect to carry the old man into this new life, and please God. It didn't work for Israel, nor will it work for us. Our hearts must be fully committed to the new man we have become; and we must learn to trust God with our whole heart.

Are we going to continue to obey the leadings of the flesh (godless human nature), or are we going to crucify the old man, for good, and start living for Christ?

Unfortunately, not every believer makes the decision

to live for Christ. Some still find pleasure in sin. It tells us in Galatians 5:16, that if we walk and live habitually in the Holy Spirit (responsive to and controlled and guided by the Spirit), then we will certainly not gratify the cravings and desires of the flesh. But if we are not responsive to and controlled by the Spirit, then we will be controlled by the flesh.

The works of the flesh are evident in these: adultery, fornication, impurity, lasciviousness, idolatry, witchcraft, hatred, strife, jealousy, anger, selfishness, divisions, party spirit (factions, sects), envy, murder, drunkenness, carousing, and things such as these *(Galatians 5:19-21)*. None of these ungodly works of the flesh should be found in a believer who crucifies his flesh daily, and habitually walks and lives in the Spirit.

The presence of the Holy Ghost produces fruit that is evidenced by love, joy, peace, patience (an even temper, forbearance), kindness, goodness (benevolence), faithfulness, gentleness (meekness, humility), and self-control (self-constraint, continence).

God's Spirit living inside of us teaches us God's

ways, and shows us how to live and walk according to the leading of the Spirit.

NEW BELIEVER'S TRAINING

Much like the rigorous training new recruits receive when they enter the military (boot camp training), our training in holiness will also be rigorous and a test of our endurance. The military puts its new recruits through a number of physical challenges that test both their physical and mental endurance. Only the physically and/or mentally strong make it through basic training.

The Christian's "boot camp" training is also physically, mentally, and at times, spiritually taxing. We will be insulted, lied on, mistreated, abused, and ostracized, because of our faith. We will lose friends, and have to endure a daily barrage of fiery darts being thrown at us by the devil. Critics will be many, and friends few. But be encouraged, Jesus also experienced these things, and more. But it didn't destroy Him; it only propelled Him into His destiny. He overcame them all.

And just look where He is today—seated at the right hand of God!

If we can endure the tests and trials of life, our reward will be great in heaven. Condition yourself to walk in holiness. Much like an athlete who conditions and trains a muscle to become strong, we can also condition and train ourselves to become strong in our faith, no longer giving in to every temptation to sin. Be strong and courageous; and fight the good fight of faith.

GROW YOUR FAITH

> BE STRONG AND COURAGEOUS.

Certain reptiles, such as snakes, go through a process called *molting*, where they "shed their skin." The snake's skin does not generally grow with it so by shedding its skin it allows for growth and the removal of existing parasites.

The Bible instructs us to lay aside every unnecessary weight and the sin that so easily entangles us so that we can run this Christian race with patient endurance, looking away from all that will distract us, and unto Jesus who is the leader and the source of our faith. We must lay aside everything that can hinder our walk with God, and keep us from living up to our full potential in Christ.

Just as the snake sheds its old skin, we must also shed our old selves so that we can grow into spiritual maturity. Stretch out of that old, dead skin which has been hampering your spiritual growth, and robe yourself in righteousness.

Grow your faith daily in the word. The more you know about God through His word, the more you will come to love Him. The more you love Him, the more you will trust Him. And the more you trust Him, the more He'll be able to use you to do great things for Him on earth.

Jesus gave His disciples hands-on training when He walked with them on earth. He taught them about the Father, and about the kingdom of God. The disciples saw God's manifested glory through Jesus. They were able to experience the fullness of God's power and anointing first-hand through Jesus. So when the trials and the persecutions came, they weren't afraid because they knew the size of the God that lived inside of them. They knew that God was more powerful than anything the enemy could throw at them.

Know the God that lives inside of you. Become acquainted with His power and anointing. Spend time in His presence, where He can impart into you spiritual wisdom, joy, love, and peace. As you grow into holiness, your faith will also begin to grow. And when your faith is strong, *nothing* will be impossible for you!

קְדוּשָׁה
HOLINESS

Chapter 14

SPIRITUAL FOOD AND SPIRITUAL FAMINE

SPIRITUAL FOOD

"For the kingdom of God is not eating and drinking, but righteousness and peace and joy in the Holy Spirit. For he who in this way serves Christ is acceptable to God and approved by men" *(Romans 14:17-18)*.

Jesus had many debates with the Pharisees. The Pharisees were an ancient Jewish sect who taught strict observance of Jewish traditions, and adherence to the laws. They prided themselves on being good Jews who followed the letter of the law (i.e. praying, fasting, religious observances, etc.). They were faithful Jews. But Jesus said they were full of hypocrisy. Their devotion to the Jewish traditions and laws was not because they loved God, but because they loved the praise of men. The Pharisees did all of these things to be seen of men—to be perceived as more righteous than others. They loved the best seats in the synagogues, the seats of honor at banquets, long greetings in the marketplace, and being called "Rabbi" by men.

However, although the Pharisees followed the letter of the law, they disregarded the more weightier matters of the law: justice, mercy, and faithfulness. In other words, they were so consumed with elevating their external appearance before men that they placed little to no thought in the condition of their hearts. Jesus said to them, "you strain at a gnat, and swallow a camel" *(Matthew 23:24)*. Whenever we get too caught up in legalism (strict, literal, or excessive conformity to the law), we miss the true nature of godliness.

The true nature of godliness is having a pure heart before God. It's not necessarily the "external" look of holiness that pleases God—although, I do believe there is a *look* of holiness, and it doesn't look anything like the world; it looks like God. Holiness starts in the heart and manifests itself outwardly. When your heart has been changed people will be able to look at you and see your pure heart and the divine glow of holiness, which changes your outward appearance.

In holiness, we no longer desire to emulate the world; we desire godliness over worldliness. That being said, we can take off our make-up and jewelry (as some churches require of their members), and still not be in right-standing with God. If our hearts are still connected to the world, an external appearance devoid of make-up and jewelry is of little benefit. God looks at our hearts. And if our hearts are not pure, He knows.

Anyone who has been in holiness for any length of

time eventually learns how to look the part. We have all but mastered the lingo: "God is good, all the time!" We've learned how to say the right things, and when to say them. We even have the mannerisms and the facial expressions mastered—the contorted face that gives us the appearance of being "deep" or "spiritual."

Some may even give up eating meat (pork, specifically) because they feel it is unclean and, therefore, might contaminate their bodies. These people are under the impression that giving up meat will keep their temples clean. Therefore, they place great spiritual value in watching what they eat. But Jesus said it is not what we take into our bodies that contaminates us, rather what comes out of us contaminates us *(Mark 7:15)*.

So then, the things we should be pursuing in God are not the external, temporary things, but rather the things that make for peace and the building up of one another—not tearing down. We tear down the work of God by trivializing it into the shallow and superficial world of legalism, causing it to be less effective and more about the natural works of man, rather than the spiritual works of God.

Jesus said, "my meat is to do the will of him that sent me, and to finish his work." Jesus' nourishment came from a spiritual place. It wasn't the natural food that sustained Him. God sustained Jesus in the spiritual when He dedicated His life to God in service. His spirit man was being fed when He accomplished God's will. When we dedicate our lives to God and accomplish His will, we will receive the nourishment we need from on high.

SPIRITUAL FAMINE

In the natural, there are often seasons of famine where there is a lack of natural food. This season could be caused by things such as drought, crop failure, or diseases, resulting in a period where nothing grows. This can be particularly devastating, especially for those who have not taken precautions to store up provisions during the seasons of plenty.

Similarly, a spiritual famine occurs when we fail to

adequately prepare ourselves in the "plentiful years" for the "lean years" that are sure to come. We might naturally assume that just because things are going well, that they will always be well. We fail to realize that just like there are dry seasons in the natural, there will also be dry seasons in our spiritual lives.

At some point, we will all experience seasons of persecution, drought, and the tests and trials that come to try our faith. But by being mindful to keep up a steady stream of prayer, fasting, and studying God's word, we keep our spiritual man well-fed, thereby, healthy and prepared for those times when the storms of life come.

The kingdom of God is truly not in natural food, which, although it gives nourishment to the body, it does very little for our souls. Our nourishment should be spiritual in nature, which gives us everlasting nourishment and strengthens us to do the work of the kingdom. We are kingdom people who have been sent to earth for a season to fulfill God's purpose on earth. Our final destination is heaven. Therefore, we should not become too attached to this world, as it is only temporary and we are just passing through.

If you find yourself in a spiritual famine, do something about it! Don't just sit there and die in it. Even the four leprous men realized they needed to do something about their current situation, lest they die *(2 Kings 7)*. There was a famine in the city. And because they were lepers and considered unclean, they were not permitted to enter the city. As they sat outside the city gate they said, "why sit we here until we die?" They knew that even if they entered the city, they might die because of the famine. But, if they continued to sit at the gate, they might also die there. So they decided to attach themselves to the camp of the Syrians.

As the four lepers entered the Syrian camp, they discovered that it had been abandoned. God had caused the Syrians to hear a noise, which they presumed to be their enemies coming to overtake them; so they fled. When the lepers entered the deserted camp, they found food, clothing, silver, and gold; suddenly, they had come upon a windfall. But, had they never made a decision to do something about their situation, more than likely they would have died of famine while they sat by the city gate.

Do not continue to sit idle and allow your spiritual famine to kill you spiritually. Get up and do something about it. Build yourself back up spiritually by feasting on the word of God. The word has life-sustaining properties. Those who hunger and thirst after righteousness shall be filled.

The Lord told the prophet Amos that there will come a time when He will send a famine in the land. But this famine will not be a famine where there is an absence of food or water. This famine will come about from a lack of hearing the words of the Lord. At this time, people will go from shore to shore seeking the word of the Lord, but they will not find it. This absence of God's word on the earth will cause a famine greater than any natural famine man has ever seen *(Amos 8)*.

When God's word is absent from our lives, it causes a famine in our souls. But there is sustenance in the word of God. Therefore, the Bible warns us against the misuse of food, and reminds us that there is more to life than food and drink. The Lord humbled Israel in the wilderness and tested them, allowing them to go hungry, and feeding them with manna from on high. This was done, the Bible says, so that they would know that man does not live by bread alone, but by every word that proceeds out of the mouth of the Lord *(Deuteronomy 8:3)*.

God is our source of life; our sustenance comes directly from Him. Our spiritual food (the word of God) should compel us to do the will of the Lord who sent us.

Chapter 15

A SIGNIFICANT SACRIFICE

God required Israel to bring a sacrifice for their sins before they could approach Him—before they would be made acceptable by Him. God instructed Israel to bring Him only their best. Israel's sacrifices to God had to be without any defects, and they had to be taken from the herd or the flocks. The grain they brought to Him had to be of the best quality, seasoned with salt but no leaven or sweetener could be added in. All of Israel's sacrifices had to be prepared according to God's specifications and standards. They were not to bring Him anything that had been torn in the field by a wild beast. (Today, we would call this road kill.) God does not want leftovers or sloppy seconds. He has always given us His best, so why would He expect anything less from us in return?

A sacrifice is only a sacrifice when it costs you something. King David said, "I will not offer burnt offerings to the Lord my God which cost me nothing" *(2 Samuel 24:24)*. Araunah, the Jebusite, was prepared to *give* the king his threshing floor—a large smooth floor, either indoor or outdoor, where they threshed the grain for harvest—and oxen so that David could sacrifice to the Lord to stop the plague that God had sent upon the people because of David's sin. But David was not willing to accept this gift from Araunah. He wanted whatever he sacrificed to God to come directly from his own hand. So he purchased the items from Araunah for fifty shekels of silver. The Lord was moved by the sacrifice and the prayer, and held back the plaque from Israel.

When God asked Abraham to sacrifice his beloved son, Isaac, it was a test. This was the son Abraham and his wife, Sarah, had prayed for. He was the *promised son*. So, I'm sure it must have been difficult in the beginning for Abraham to understand why God was now asking him to kill Isaac. But Abraham trusted God. And if God had been so gracious as to give him a son, then surely he could give that son back to God. And because Abraham was willing to sacrifice his best, God provided a ram in the bush, and spared Isaac *(Genesis 22:1-13)*.

What are you willing to sacrifice to the Lord? What are you willing to give up in order to gain eternal life? Or,

> WHAT ARE YOU WILLING TO SACRIFIE TO THE LORD?

are you like most people today who don't want to give up anything, but hold on to everything while still trying to serve God? This is almost like holding something in each hand with both fists tightly clinched, and trying to grab for something else at the same time. You will never be able to grab the thing you're reaching for until you release what is in your hands. Let go of the world so that you can gain heaven.

Many of our brethren in the faith lost their lives because of the gospel. John the Baptist was beheaded in prison by Herod because of a promise Herod had made to Herodias' daughter. It is reported that all of the Apostles, except John, were killed by martyrdom. The world wanted to stop this gospel about Jesus Christ from spreading; so they thought that if they killed His followers, it would squash the movement. But it did not, because over two thousand years later Christianity is still alive and well. The gospel is still being preached, and lives are still being saved.

Jesus was *willing* to lay down His life for the cause of saving that which had been lost in the fall of man, and restoring it back to God. Those who are not willing to sacrifice everything to follow Jesus are not worthy to be called His disciples. A true disciple does not turn back at the first sign of trouble. A true disciple is willing to stick with you until the end. A sacrifice is only a sacrifice if it costs you something. Make sure your sacrifice to God is significant, and from the heart.

PRAYER

I've often heard prayer described in many ways: a weapon that defeats the enemy; a way to get a response from God; a way to communicate with God. And, "Prayer is the key; faith unlocks the door."

What we know from the Scriptures is that Jesus prayed often. He would often get away to a secret place, or to a mountain to pray. Jesus remained in constant communication with God through prayer. I believe, through prayer, that He was receiving strength and encouragement for His mission, and being empowered to fulfill the Scriptures, which prophesy of Him.

Jesus was also setting an example for His disciples to follow. He knew that He would soon be leaving them and that when He did, the disciples would need to talk to Him through prayer, as He often talked to the Father. Jesus had given His disciples a mission, and through prayer He would be able to direct them in this mission, strengthening them and encouraging them along the way.

It's not always easy for us to set aside time to pray, especially when we have committed ourselves to so many other things. And, our flesh doesn't always want to pray. But prayer is a necessary part of a Christian's walk with Christ. When we pray, we are strengthened in our faith, and become closer to God in our hearts. It's nearly impossible to not know someone with whom you converse with everyday. If you want to get to know God, talk to Him everyday. God will begin to reveal Himself to you through prayer, and you will begin to form a bond that is not easily broken.

I've discovered that when you set aside time everyday to pray, you begin to look forward to this time, and will move aside any hindrances that may get in the way of your spending time with God. But the most amazing thing I've discovered about meeting God everyday in prayer is that He also looks forward to spending time with you!

This time, however, should *not* be spent whining and complaining to God, or constantly asking Him for material things. Prayer should be a time for you to strengthen your bond with God. It's a time to thank Him for His goodness, and His mercy, and for the love He's shown you over the years. And prayer is also a time for you to just worship Him for who He is. How would you feel if every time you talked with someone all they did was complain, or ask you for money? You would quickly sour of them, and probably do everything you could to avoid them.

We should not treat God like an ATM, or a punching bag. He knows the things we have need of. I'm not saying we should never make our needs known to God. But when we *only* talk to Him when we need something, it can look as if we only serve Him because of the benefits we think we can get from Him. And when we constantly whine and complain to Him it gives the impression that we don't really trust Him to meet our needs, as He said He would in His word.

From my experience, God will sometimes meet the

needs and desires of your heart, automatically, and out of love, during your time of fellowship in prayer. There have been times during prayer when, while I was just worshiping God, that He would speak to my heart an answer to a problem that had been on my heart. Or, He would direct me to a certain place where I would find a certain item that I'd been desiring, but never having actually prayed to Him about. But He knew the desire was there; and because He's such a wonderful God, He would speak to me in prayer directing me to the very thing I had been desiring. He just amazes me that way. He *knows* what we have need of, and desires to give us the desires of our hearts as long as we are sincere toward Him and love Him with our whole hearts.

So, don't neglect prayer, which is our time to be alone with God, that He so graciously grants to us. He desires to spend time with us. And we are enriched by time spent with Him. Jesus prayed often, and so should we.

HUMILITY

God places great value in a humble heart—a heart that is not puffed up with one's own self-worth; but one that is fully surrendered to God, and acknowledges that there is no one greater than Him. God resists the proud and gives grace to the humble.

To serve God, we must sacrifice our own sense of self-worth or our need to feel important, because, let's face it, where were *we* when God created the heaven and the earth? Or when He spoke to the stars, the moon, and the sun, commanding them to take their place in the sky and to give light to the earth - were we there? Or were we there when God formed man out of the dust of the ground, and breathed into his nostrils the breath of life, making him a living soul? We came from dust, and when we die we will return back to dust. But God has always been and will forever be.

Pride has been the downfall of many men. They became puffed up, their egos were inflated, and it blinded them to the truth staring them in the face (that they were nothing compared to God). They became too full of themselves and overly confident in their own abilities, intelligence, and sense of worth. These prideful men thought they were superhuman, or invincible. When we become full of ourselves, we become blind and vulnerable to the destructive forces of Satan. The person who is full of pride usually self-destructs. No one can help a proud man, or keep him from falling on his own sword. Pride is a deadly emotion. Avoid it at all costs.

OBEDIENCE

Obey God, keep His commandments, love your neighbor as you love yourself: This is what God asks of us. A heart that is not obedient is a heart that is out of the will of God. Israel refused to obey God and to keep His commandments, and because of this, many of them died in the wilderness. These, unfortunately, never made it to the promised land.

This is what often perplexes me. Israel saw God's power when He delivered them from Egyptian bondage with a mighty hand. They saw His glory when He showed

Himself to them in the wilderness. Israel experienced God's provision when He fed them with manna, and when He preserved their clothes from wearing out for forty years. They lived under His protection when He shielded them from their enemies. Israel experienced God's power first-hand, and yet they still refused to serve Him and to remain faithful to Him.

They persistently and stubbornly served other gods, and murmured and complained against God in the wilderness. This stirred up God's anger, causing Him to pour out His wrath upon them. In fact, had it not been for Moses' intervention, God very well may have destroyed them all in the wilderness. But God, always one to honor His word and to keep His covenant, remembered His covenant with Abraham and, thus, spared a remnant of Abraham's seed to live on and continue his legacy, which fulfilled the promise He made to Abraham to bless his seed and to make them as innumerable as the sand by the seashore.

Our obedience causes us to receive a blessing from the Lord. Disobedience brings a curse. If you feel that your life is under a curse—whether it's a generational curse or a demonic curse—check to see if somewhere in your life (past or present) there is a history of disobedience to God that may have opened the door to a curse.

Do you feel that the hand of God has been removed from over your life? Are you living in obedience to Him, or are you living to please yourself? Pray for a heart of obedience so that God's hand of protection will always cover and protect you and your family.

Holiness requires a sacrifice from each of us; and that sacrifice must be significant. It is this sacrifice that releases us to move closer to God. When we are willing to release, sometimes the things we hold dear, it shows our love for God and our complete devotion to Him. The person who is not willing to sacrifice everything to follow God does not fully love Him; because when we *really* love Him, we are willing to lay down everything to serve Him. Make sure your sacrifice to God is significant.

Chapter 16

THE CHURCH

The Church is collectively made up of a body of believers who come together under the banner of one common faith. This faith is belief in the Lord and Creator of the universe (Jehovah), and in Jesus Christ the Messiah, who came to earth born of a virgin and in the form of human flesh to take away the sins of the world. There is salvation in no other name, than the name of Jesus Christ.

The Bible makes an analogy between a human body, which is comprised of many parts (a head, arms, legs, feet), and the church. Though there are many members, there is only one body. Each individual body part needs to work together as one unit in order for the body to function properly. Each individual part, being unique on its own, collectively forms a whole.

The church, which is also made up of many members (pastor, elders, laypersons), forms one body. As with the human body, every member of the church needs to work together as one cohesive unit for the church body to function accordingly.

If the feet, wanting to go their own way, refuse to follow the body, you end up with one stumbling-bumbling mess. The feet were not designed to go in one direction while the body goes in another. For the body to work in the way it was designed, all of its members have to work together in perfect harmony. This is also true for the church body.

When Jesus left the earth to return to glory after

His resurrection, He left behind a church that was fully operational and unified.

On the day of Pentecost, the church was together in the upper room and on one accord waiting for a move of God, which had been prophesied by the Prophet Joel *(Joel 2:28-29)*. They were all gathered together this day in the upper room because Jesus had told them to wait in Jerusalem for the promise of the Father—the gift of the Holy Ghost.

When the Holy Ghost fell on the day of Pentecost, it was unlike anything anyone had ever seen before. The Spirit of God touched every believer in the place with great

> **THE SPIRIT OF GOD TOUCHED EVERY BELIEVER IN THE PLACE.**

demonstration and power so that those who saw and heard it were pricked in their hearts, and believed on the God in whom the disciples worshiped. God's power was manifested this day through the in-filling of the Holy Ghost as the disciples began to prophesy and speak with tongues as the Spirit gave the utterance *(Acts*

2).

This must have been a marvelous sight to behold. Cloven tongues sitting upon each of them. The sound of a rushing mighty wind filling the whole house. And a miraculous sound as the sound of a chorus of angels speaking and singing in the most beautiful and melodic heavenly language. This scene exemplifies the Lord's holy will for the church—to be an earthly, visual representation of heaven.

> **THE CHURCH IS TO REPRESENT GOD ON THE EARTH.**

The church is to represent God on the earth. We are an extension of Him: His grace, power, love, and majesty. This is what Jesus did when He walked the earth in human form. He humbled Himself and took on human flesh, and became the visual image of the invisible God. Jesus' life was an example for the church to follow. His was a life of obedience to God: Prayer. Fasting. Healing Sick. Casting out Demons. Teaching. Preaching. Correcting. Encouraging. And He told His disciples, and ultimately us today, "greater works than these shall you do" *(John 14:12)*.

Jesus did all of these things while physically embodying human flesh, by the power of the Holy Ghost—as He was also filled with the Holy Ghost *(Luke 3:22)*. Jesus operated by faith. He had faith in the power of God. His faith in God caused Him to perform many miracles. He resisted the temptation to sin against God. He walked the earth directing all men to give glory to God, while deflecting praise away from Himself. God sent, in Jesus, a living, breathing example for the church to follow. It was something *tangible* that we could see and grab hold of and apply to our own lives.

When you follow the life and progression of Jesus' ministry, you see Him healing the sick everywhere He goes. If He perceived in His spirit that someone had the faith to be healed, He healed them. There were, however, times when individuals were not healed because of their lack of faith. For example, Jesus came into His own country and "could there do no mighty work, save that he laid his hands upon a few sick folk, and healed them" *(Mark 6:5)*. Jesus was amazed at the level of their unbelief.

Jesus repeatedly said that He came to earth to do the will of the Father who sent Him. He makes it very clear through His actions that it is God's will to heal everyone who has the faith to be healed.

When God brought Israel forth out of Egypt, not one of them was feeble *(Psalm 105:37)*. The Lord expressly wants His people to be physically well. We have been given authority and power through Jesus to lay hands on the sick so that they are healed. But if we ourselves are often sick, how effective can we be in helping others receive their healing? People would have a much easier time believing God for their healing if our own lives visually reflected God's will.

Our minds also must be sharp and alert, free from an overload of negative energies. We need to be assertive everyday about filling our minds with good things, rather than loading them down with junk. "Finally, brethren, whatsoever things are true, whatsoever things are honest, whatsoever things are just, whatsoever things are pure, whatsoever things are lovely, whatsoever things are of good report; if there be any virtue, and if there be any praise, think on these things" *(Philippians 4:8)*. Meditate daily on the word of God, which provides healing for your mind.

The church's spiritual health should also be on par with God's will. Again, when Jesus left the earth He left behind a church that was fully functioning and operating under the power and the anointing of God. Unfortunately, the church today does not look anything like the early church. Instead of a church where powerful manifestations and supernatural miracles are the norm, today's modern church looks more like a wasteland where weak, powerless Christians reside.

The church has been infiltrated by false doctrines. And in some cases, we've handed over our power to the enemy. Most Christians rarely read the Bible, and have only a basic knowledge of God, and His word. We've become more accustomed today to hearing a weak, watered-down version of the gospel, that we no longer want to hear spiritual truth. We often want to hear more about God's love, grace, and forgiveness, while rejecting preaching on God's judgment of sin.

This light, fluffy version of the gospel makes us feel good and accepted by God no matter the condition of our souls, and no matter how often we repeatedly sin against Him, and disobey His commandments. But the truth, even though it isn't as easy for us to digest, must be preached for it is God's word. It's the truth that is like holding up a mirror to our face and showing us what we *really* look like to God; it reveals our true heart condition. Truth will sometimes make us squirm in our seats, as it is not always comfortable when we see ourselves through the lens of truth. No, it doesn't always feel good, but it is absolutely necessary to produce godliness.

The Apostle Paul said that the church of the living God is the pillar and support of the truth *(1 Timothy 3:15)*. We, therefore, must embrace God's truth while rejecting false doctrine. But in order to embrace truth, we must first know what it is. The only way to become acquainted with truth is through the word of God. It is very easy for a person to be deceived when he or she does not have a full understanding of God and His word.

This is how false prophets and false doctrines gain access into the church. These deceivers start by twisting the word a little here and there. In the beginning, it's very subtle, just like the serpent when he said to Eve, "you shall not surely die if you eat of the tree that is in the middle of the garden. For God knows that in the day you eat from it your eyes will be opened, and you will become as gods, knowing good and evil." This was all it took for Eve to start questioning what she knew God had told her (not to eat from the tree). When she began to listen to the serpent, it caused her to start looking at the *tree of the knowledge of good and evil* differently from that moment on. And we all know what happened next: she took that fatal bite. And in the moment she ate of the fruit from the forbidden tree, she died a spiritual death, which, in my opinion, is a death worse than physical death (for a Christian). Eve's act of disobedience caused a spiritual separation from God.

Knowing God's word will prevent us from being deceived by the wicked one; because, when he approaches us in his ever-so-subtle, sneaky way we will immediately reject him because we know what God's word says. And when a false prophet makes his way into the pulpit and starts twisting the word of God, we will reject it because we know that anyone who adds to or takes anything away from the word of God is against Him. Do not be deceived. Stand firm on the word and reject all manner of lies and hypocrisy, no matter the source.

The church is a spiritual organism. It is a living, breathing representation of God Himself. The church has been imbibed with God's Spirit. Everything the church does should mirror God's eternal nature. The church is the tangible, physical evidence of God's existence. God works in conjunction with His church to fulfill His will on earth. We touch heaven through the spiritual realm. We receive our instructions from God through the Holy Ghost. The Bible is our primary reference manual, given us by God for the church's edification and instruction *(2 Timothy 3:16).*

When we are born-again we no longer belong to ourselves, but to God. When we take the step over into salvation we are telling God, "yes, I am willing to represent you on earth. And I sacrifice my will for yours." We then, in a spiritual sense, give up the rights to own our selves when we become born-again believers. We've been bought and sealed by the blood of Jesus Christ. Our lives should now reflect our new spiritual birth.

Our new identity in Christ should be visible in our day-to-day lives. Our conversations should be different. When people who knew us prior to salvation see us, they should immediately be able to detect that a change has taken place in us. People should be drawn to us by the light of Christ that radiates through us, and as a result, this light should in turn point them to God.

God has great expectations for His church. He expects us to walk in faith, and in the power and anointing of the Holy Ghost, and to be a reflection of His glory on earth. We should strive to be like Christ in all that we do. We should strive for holiness, for God Himself is holy.

TODAY'S CHURCH

I believe that God is greatly concerned about the condition the church is in today. Somewhere along the way we've gotten off-track; we've lost our way. The church has not always held firm to God; we have often neglected Him and His ways. The church has become divided and split into differing denominations and organizations. We've established these denominations and organizations along various doctrinal statements, which we give great credence to. We identify ourselves according to our specific doctrinal beliefs, when we should be identifying ourselves with God.

Some even elevate and revere certain apostles, saints, and biblical figures, to the point where these individuals are worshiped in place of God. We put more focus on the *created,* rather than the *Creator*. This goes back to man's need to have a visible, tangible object or person to worship. A carnal man finds it difficult to worship an invisible God, who must be worshiped on a spiritual level. We prefer to worship God in the natural, which is much easier for us to understand with our natural senses. In order to elevate ourselves to the spiritual we must crucify the flesh, which cannot understand the things of God because they are spiritual and eternal in the heavens.

God is not like us. Therefore, we should resist the urge to place God on our same level. We must follow Him and obey His leading. He is our God and we are His people. Our life, sustenance, and purpose comes from God.

> HE IS OUR GOD AND WE ARE HIS PEOPLE.

It's becoming evident that a good majority of Christians today don't really know God. We go to church every Sunday, and may occasionally make it to Bible Study during the week. We sing in the choir, usher, and give our tithes and offerings faithfully, but we still haven't gone past a head-knowledge of God—having yet to receive a personal revelation of Him, and to experience Him in all of His fullness. Most Christians have been wading in the shallow waters, and have yet to explore the deep things of God. There's so much depth in God yet to be discovered. Don't be content with the shallow things of God; dive in head-first and explore the depths of God; you'll be amazed!

Our reluctance to become intimately acquainted with God has made it difficult for us to worship Him. We sing songs about Him, but it hasn't become real or personal to us. As praise and worship goes forth, we participate, but our worship experience is often on a shallow, surface level where we are often left distant and aloof from God. There is a barrier standing between us and God.

Very recently, I attended a particular church. And prior to going to this church, I already had a certain expectation in my mind of the type of service I might find there, although I had never visited this church before. Because it was an "ethnic" church I expected the service to be lively. Sometimes we expect certain groups to be more expressive in their worship as they are naturally, culturally more expressive people. But when I got to the church I didn't find a lively worship service at all; they were actually quite reserved. This church was not very demonstrative in their worship as I had anticipated, but rather laid back and often void of emotion.

And as the service progressed, I began to get a revelation of why this is. I saw that although many of them sang the songs, they didn't really know God; they were basically just going through the motions. And I could sense that people were distracted. Although their bodies were there at the church, their minds were elsewhere: possibly on their plans for later that day, or on what they were going to prepare for dinner. And more and more today, we find that people have become quite addicted to their smartphones, and with what's going on in *social media land*. Some will even sit there in church paying more attention to their phones than to what's going on in the moment—namely, the praise and worship of God. We've become too distracted. And I sensed a distraction in this church on this day.

Unfortunately, this is becoming more common in our churches today. We are often distant from God, and distracted. Most Christians, sadly, don't know the

God they claim to serve. And how can we worship Him when we don't know Him intimately? Our knowledge of Him, unfortunately, is not often based on personal experience, but rather on what we've heard about Him across the pulpit, or the stories we've heard in Sunday School.

Often, we think we're worshiping God when we're really worshiping the music. We've fallen in love with the rhythm of the music, and how it makes us feel. The music makes us want to sway to the beat, and tap our feet. And sometimes, our movements often betray us. We can easily forget we're in church worshiping a holy God, and unconsciously slip in a move that we would normally reserve for the dance floor (yes, unfortunately, some Christians still go to the clubs), or when we're listening to a slow jam on the radio. Some people just get lost in the music, but they quickly catch themselves when they remember where they are, and quickly change their movements to a more "church-y" move, or at least one that they feel is more appropriate for church. But some just keep right on snapping their fingers, and gyrating to the beat.

My point is, the focus is not where it should be — on God. The focus is on the music, which we can better relate to. True worship places the focus on God. When we think about how great our God is, and when we try and comprehend how such a great God could love a people as unworthy as we are, it makes us humbled in His presence. It almost makes us want to weep.

When we read in the Bible about people who have had personal encounters with God, we see that these people were barely able to stand in the presence of a holy God. The light of His glory alone was enough to take the strength out of them, bringing them to their knees before Him in awestruck worship. These people recognized that they were in the presence of the living God, and that they were not worthy to be there. They often bowed themselves to the ground, or were stunned to silence, unable to speak. When God's presence shows up, we become lowly before Him.

This is what the *Azusa* worshipers experienced in their times of worship; their testimonies were that they became as grasshoppers in God's presence. They suddenly became aware of their nothingness as they became humbled in the presence of the true and living God. Being in God's presence is a sobering, humbling experience.

This is what the church needs today — an encounter with the living God. We've become too full of self. We've become prideful of our "place" in Christ, as if by some goodness of our own we have been placed there. None of us were worthy enough to die for our own sins, bringing about our salvation. Only the blood of Jesus could save us from sin. We owe Him the honor and the praise because had it not been for Him we would still be lost.

The church today has also become blind to the state of its true condition. We often think that we are more spiritual or more anointed than we really are. We want to move and operate in the spiritual gifts of God, but we don't want to humble ourselves before Him and receive from Him. Often, we want God to follow our leading, thinking we know best. But in order to walk in the fullness of God's spiritual gifts, we must be filled with the Holy Ghost—which is another thing we want our way.

We want God to fill us up with all of His power and anointing, but we don't want to step out of the way and allow Him to do it. We want to be in control even of how He fills us with *His* Spirit. I've even seen some try and make up their own "tongues," instead of allowing God to give them the utterance. We think that we, never having been to heaven, can make up our own "heavenly language." This is arrogance, and ignorance. We've become blind to the truth. We've been taught lies and falsehoods, and have believed them; and these lies have become our doctrine. The Holy Ghost comes from God. He fills us with His Spirit when we humble ourselves and receive of Him. Be sensitive to the Spirit of God, and allow Him to work in your life.

One Sunday, as I was getting ready for church, the Lord laid it on my heart to stop by this particular church's 9 o'clock service. I wondered why God was sending me there; but I soon discovered why once I got to the church. When the pastor got up to preach, he started sharing with the church how he was recently at a certain restaurant, and struck up a conversation with the waitress. The waitress began to open up and share with him some of the things she was going through in her personal life. Apparently, she knew he was a pastor and felt comfortable sharing.

While the pastor told the congregation that he didn't want to pray with the waitress right there in the restaurant because he felt it might be inappropriate, he said that he did pray for her when he got home and felt very strongly that God was going to turn her situation around in response to the prayer. He said that he wanted to go back to the restaurant and follow-up with this waitress and ask her how things were going for her now, fully believing that God had already begun to turn her situation around. But what I really heard this pastor saying was that he was *afraid* to pray for the waitress right there in the restaurant because they were in a public place and he was either afraid of offending people, or uncertain of what they might say. (Note to self: don't ever ask this pastor to pray for you; his faith is weak; no boldness.)

The pastor then proceeded to tell the congregation that he thinks we can be bold for God—apparently his boldness is reserved for when he's within the four walls of the church—without being "weird" about it. To illustrate his point, he paused for a moment as three guys took to the stage to perform a brief "skit." The skit was about two guys who were trying to lead their unsaved friend to the Lord. One of the two guys was really zealous for the Lord, as he was portraying the "weird" one. This guy was witnessing to his unsaved friend with a high-pitched voice, using a lot of Christian "jargon," and loudly praying for this poor guy, who appeared to be in shock or possibly afraid because of the overzealousness of his two friends.

This skit continued for about five minutes. The congregation was highly amused, and you could hear laughter rippling throughout the church—they were clearly entertained by all this. But as I sat there watching this all unfold my spirit became very grieved, and heavy. I heard the Lord say, *"do you see what they're doing in my house?"* I'm sure the shock and alarm of what I was witnessing must have registered on my face. But, I clearly heard God speak to me, and my spirit was very heavy.

God, however, was *not* amused by the skit, and He takes very seriously the things that we do in His house. My spirit was very heavy when I left this church. Later, in the wee hours of the night, as I began to pray and talk to God about it (because my spirit was still heavy), I said to Him: *I really think the pastor's heart was in the right place; he was just trying to find a way to get his point across to the congregation. But I really don't think he meant any harm by it; he's just...well, ignorant. And, Lord, I don't think they knew that what they were doing was offending you.* And I began to pray for the pastor: that his eyes would be opened; and that he would have discernment to know when God is not pleased. I really do think his actions were sincere; but what matters most is what God thinks.

God takes very seriously the things we do in His house. We have to be very careful not to offend God with our actions. The things *we* think are entertaining and funny are not necessarily entertaining and funny to God. We can very easily cross a line without even knowing it. And if we are not spiritually discerning, we can miss the mood of God in that very moment when He is letting us *know* that He is not pleased. I pray that the church today has discernment to know when we are crossing a line, and when God is not pleased with us so that we can quickly change our actions.

I try and always put myself in a position to talk to God, and where He can talk to me. And God has been showing me lately what He desires for the church. (His expectations for us are high.) And I often pray and intercede on the behalf of the church, and my fellow Christians. I pray a lot for God's mercy: that He would not remove His mercy from us. God really is trying to get our attention; I just pray that we would always listen and obey.

There was another occasion when God sent me to a church out of town. When I arrived at the church, I noticed that almost everybody there was wearing pink.

And when I walked through the doors of the sanctuary, the usher handed me a small pamphlet, which I didn't read until after I had been seated.

Apparently, everyone in the church was wearing pink this day in support of *Breast Cancer Awareness.* And the pamphlet the usher handed me was an informational pamphlet about breast cancer. Once I saw this, I knew almost immediately why God had sent me there.

While we gladly support and are happy for those who have survived breast cancer, the church should not have more faith in medical science than we have in God. The world is looking for a cure for breast cancer, but the church already has a cure. And if we were operating in faith and in the power of the Holy Ghost, we would be doing what we have been commissioned to do—lay hands on the sick so that they will be healed. But we must have faith to do this.

The early church had faith. Jesus had faith. They believed in the power of God, and knew that they had been called to administer His power on the earth. These warriors of faith laid hands on the sick wherever they went, and the sick were healed. I'm sure these people did not walk past the people in their churches who were bound by sickness and disease. Nor did they provide wheelchairs and walkers for these people, or set up "deaf ministries" in the church. When we do these things we are operating outside of God's will.

I attended a church that went on a missions trip to Africa every year. I was very happy to hear this, and wanted to learn more about these trips. I thought that I might want to accompany them on one of these trips, and I began to earnestly pray about it. As time passed, I noticed that I hadn't received confirmation from God that He wanted me to go on this trip (I believe in talking to God about everything).

In the meantime, this church was planning their next missions trip to Africa and started holding informational meetings about the trip, and it's itinerary. As I sat in on these informational meetings, my eyes began to open. I heard about medical clinics, supplies, field trips, and a women's empowerment conference. They were even talking about taking over a used wheelchair and walkers for the people there. Well, based on what God had been showing me in His word about His will as it relates to healing, I knew that this was outside of His will, and that I personally could not be a part of this type of program without offending God.

How could I stand in support of a program that was designed to "keep" people in bondage (whether done out of ignorance or not), when I clearly knew God's will, and what He expects of His people? But, sadly, our faith has become weak and we have decided that if it's God's will to heal someone, then *He* would heal them; and if people are not healed, then we think that it must not have been God's will. But our spiritual eyes have become dim, and we are unable to see the other side of the equation where God is waiting on us to do what He's already commissioned us to do. This is why we often hear prayers prayed in the church asking *God* to go into the hospitals and touch the sick and dying, when God is saying, no, I told *you* to go! The church has forgotten its purpose.

God didn't just save us for ourselves alone. He

saved us so that we would preach the gospel to the lost, offer hope to the hopeless, and set those who have been bound by the enemy free from their bondage, in the name of Jesus Christ. The church has gotten way off track. We've become more carnally minded than we are spiritually minded. And we lack faith—which displeases God.

I know what I'm saying is going against all that we have been taught, and all that we have come to believe. But if our beliefs aren't based on Scripture they are not truth, no matter how strongly we believe them. God wants His church full of the Holy Ghost, and operating in faith according to His will for us.

We represent God. We are in the world, but we are not *of* the world. God's church does not operate according to worldly-standards; God's church operates according to His standards. And His standards, and power, are far more superior to the world's. We do not go to the world in search of a cure for cancer. We know that God *is* the cure, and that He has empowered us to act on His behalf, as His representatives here on earth so that the world may see, hear, and believe.

We must be about our Father's business, because there is much work to do, and many people who need to be delivered out of Satan's evil hands. The church needs to wake up, stand up, and be who God created us to be. We are not our own. Our lives no longer belong to us. We must be willing to sacrifice our lives so that God's will is performed in the earth.

We are living in the last and evil days. The trumpet of God is soon to sound, and Jesus is about to make His appearance in the sky to call His church home. But we should not want to go alone with Him when He returns. We should want to see, not just our friends and families saved, but the whole world saved.

All those who are not following God when Christ returns for His church will not go back with Him. They will, unfortunately, have to go through great *tribulation*; and this will not be an easy period for anyone to go through. No one wants to go through seven years on this earth when God has removed His church, and His mercy from the earth.

So, if you're still in sin, stop sinning. If you haven't repented of your sins, repent today and then turn away from sin completely. Sin and disobedience will keep us outside of the will of God, where there is no protection by God, and where the sinful and the disobedient are fated to incur His wrath.

Time is short. The *Day of the Lord* is swiftly approaching. There is nothing holding back Jesus' return now, *except* God's grace and mercy. God has extended His grace and mercy to allow us, and the world, time to get it together — to come out of our sin, and to follow Him.

Why go to hell when you don't have to? Hell, which has been prepared for Satan and his angels, is now the place where all those who are outside of God's plan of salvation, or those who have turned away from Him, will be punished for eternity.

God is calling His people to holiness. He's calling us out of darkness, and into His marvelous light.

Church, get ready!

Chapter 17

MARRIAGE

Marriage, in my opinion, is one of the greatest gifts God gave to man. God, seeing Adam everyday in the garden, and realizing something was missing, said, "It's not good for man to be alone" *(Genesis 2:18)*. So God created a woman as the perfect mate for Adam. In doing so, God created in Eve a lifetime companion, best friend, confidant, and support system.

They were each uniquely designed to be the perfect mate for each other. God had purpose in mind when He designed the man and the woman.

God created marriage to be a covenant entered into willingly between male and female. The covenant is built on the foundation of love and mutual respect, and in accordance with biblical principles. Once the covenant is sealed, the two become husband and wife. A man should, therefore, leave his father and mother and cling to his wife, establishing a separate household together of their own, with the man as the head. By agreeing to this marriage, the two have now entered into a life-long marital agreement between themselves and God.

They both promise to love, honor, and cherish each other. Some couples choose to replace the word "obey" with "cherish" in their vows. Whichever one you use, you have promised to both God, and your spouse, to put your heart and soul into honoring these vows.

We know God to be a covenant-keeping God. He made a spiritual covenant with Abraham which simply stated that if Abraham obeyed all of God's commands,

God would give Abraham a son, and make him the father of many nations, and Abraham would be blessed, and his seed after him would also be blessed *(Genesis 17)*.

When God made Abraham this promise, He was willing and able to honor it. We should, therefore, only enter into contractual agreements when we feel we are fully capable of performing all of the duties stipulated in the contract.

God fulfilled His promise to Abraham by blessing him with a son (Isaac) with his wife Sarah, and Abraham became the father of many nations. Abraham's seed was indeed multiplied and became as innumerable as the sand by the sea shore *(Hebrews 11:12)*.

> **WHEN GOD MADE ABRAHAM THIS PROMISE, HE WAS WILLING AND ABLE TO HONOR IT.**

When we make the decision to enter into the covenant of marriage, we should only do so having a full understanding of what it is we are agreeing to, and feeling confident that we are able to perform all of the duties of marriage. We should always be prayerfully intentional about seeking God for the right mate. I strongly believe that God has prepared for each of us the mate that He feels is best suited for us.

Unfortunately, too many people enter into marriage lightly—having very little consideration of what it is they are entering into, and what is required of them to maintain it. They may often repeat their wedding vows as if they were simply repeating rote prayers which have been committed to memory, emitting very little emotion behind it.

God wants us all to have a wonderful marriage, filled with love and happiness for many years to come. The Bible equips us with the tools we need to have a successful marriage. This should, without question, be the first place every Christian goes in search of answers for not only a happy marriage but for all of life's issues and problems.

The Bible gives us guidelines to follow in order to have a successful marriage. A great portion of God's recipe for a good marriage can be found in Ephesians

5:22-33:

> 22 Wives, submit yourselves unto your own husbands, as unto the Lord.
>
> 23 For the husband is the head of the wife, even as Christ is the head of the church: and he is the saviour of the body.
>
> 24 Therefore as the church is subject unto Christ, so let the wives be to their own husbands in every thing.
>
> 25 Husbands, love your wives, even as Christ also loved the church, and gave himself for it;
>
> 26 That he might sanctify and cleanse it with the washing of water by the word,
>
> 27 That he might present it to himself a glorious church, not having spot, or wrinkle, or any such thing; but that it should be holy and without blemish.
>
> 28 So ought men to love their wives as their own bodies. He that loveth his wife

loveth himself.

29 For no man ever yet hated his own flesh; but nourisheth and cherisheth it, even as the Lord the church:

30 For we are members of his body, of his flesh, and of his bones.

31 For this cause shall a man leave his father and mother, and shall be joined unto his wife, and they two shall be one flesh.

32 This is a great mystery: but I speak concerning Christ and the church.

33 Nevertheless let every one of you in particular so love his wife even as himself; and the wife see that she reverence her husband.

This is a powerful text that can probably best be summarized in the following way:

- Wives, willingly submit yourselves to the authority God has given the man to be the head of your household. And if you don't feel that you can readily submit to him, then you probably shouldn't have married him in the first place. God is not asking you to submit to him because He feels that you are in any way inadequate. (To the contrary.) This is just the role God chose to give to the man, as he is to be your covering and protector, which is a role that he is naturally best suited for. So don't take it personal.

- Husbands, love your wives as you love your own bodies, giving of yourselves sacrificially in a way that produces a holy union before God. Do not seek to establish a separate family unit of your own under your parents' roof, as this will never work. When seeking to establish a household with your wife, you must leave your family's home, where your father is already the "big cheese," and create a separate household of your own, where you can now rightfully be the "big cheese" over your *own* family, thereby preventing a potential clash with your father over authority.

- Wives, show respect for your husbands, understanding the depth of the responsibility God has placed on his shoulders, and work together as one cohesive unit, both you and your husband, to make your marriage pleasing and acceptable in God's eyes. More than anything, your husband needs to feel respected by his family for the job he is dutifully performing as provider and protector. This makes him feel good; and as you well know, everyone wants to feel loved and respected. Every man needs to know that his family sees and appreciates all that he does for them.

I strongly believe that more marriages today would have a better chance of surviving if we would simply carve out a few moments every day to spend quality time with our spouse, letting them know how much we truly love and appreciate them. A little validation works wonders in a marriage.

One thing that I am convinced is almost guaranteed to destroy *any* marriage is the practice of demeaning and disrespecting your spouse, especially in public. When it's done in private it's bad, but when you demean your spouse in public for all the world to see it takes it to another level. This is because, demeaning your spouse in public tells the world that they have no worth, and are not worthy of respect. And even doing so in private sends this same message to your spouse. It is very much like taking a hatchet and chopping them up into a million little pieces. We cut them down with every swipe of our tongue. No marriage can survive this.

Think about what you are saying *before* you say it. We may lash out at our spouse in anger, in the heat of the moment, and say things we later regret. But once these words are out there, we can't ever take them back. Even if we were to apologize for them later, and make up, these words are still out there in the atmosphere forever hovering over us, waiting to implode in our marriage at any moment.

As children, we often repeated the popular children's

rhyme: "sticks and stones may break my bones, but words will never hurt me." But we quickly discovered that words do hurt. A broken bone eventually heals, but a hurtful word spoken in anger, or in jest, cuts deep into a person's soul leaving a wound that is much harder to heal. Words do hurt. And no marriage can survive very long when one party, or both, continuously lashes out at their spouse with mean, hateful words. Be kind to one another, carefully considering the other's feelings. And remember, God is always watching. And if God were to play back all of these shameful episodes in our marriage, we would probably come out looking more like the villain rather than the victim.

Nagging is another thing that has destroyed the peace and harmony in many marriages. In fact, the Bible says, "It is better to dwell in the wilderness, than with a contentious and an angry woman" *(Proverbs 21:19)*. Persistent arguing can quickly drive a wedge between husband and wife.

I remember a few years ago watching a certain "reality" television show where the cameras followed the day-to-day lives of a couple who were the parents of multiples. The family was already the proud parents of twins, when, a few years later they were surprised by the birth of sextuplets, bringing their brood to a total of eight.

As you might imagine, having so many children in such a short amount of time certainly added to the stress of what was probably already a contentious marriage. While the mom and dad were pretty good parents to the children, they didn't always appear to be very good at being husband and wife. The cameras showed a lot of escalating friction between the two.

While the husband seemed to me to be rather placid, the wife was anything but. She was a perfectionist who insisted on having things her way. And she was always right (in her mind anyway). She often treated her husband as if he were simply one of the kids instead of a co-partner, and certainly not the head of the household.

This woman had a certain way of belittling and demeaning her husband. There were a couple occasions where she lashed out at him in public. And these were the ones the viewers saw because the cameras just happened to be there at the time. But, I'm pretty sure that at this point in their marriage these episodes had already become regular occurrences.

The husband just never seemed to be able to do anything right. No matter how hard he tried, she was never satisfied and always critical of everything he did. If he folded the laundry, he didn't fold it the "right" way. If he combed the kids' hair, he could never be certain that she would be happy with the way he did that even.

One particular morning as they were getting the kids dressed, this wife became very upset with her husband when he laid the kids' clothes on the floor. In fact, she yelled at him for laying "clean" clothes on a "dirty" floor, then proceeded to snatch the clothes up off the floor, and lay them on the sofa and commenced to dressing the kids herself, all the while scolding him for his carelessness. "Didn't he know how hard she worked to keep the kids' clothes clean?"

But I couldn't help but notice that no sooner had she finished dressing the kids herself, that the kids went right back and sat down on the "dirty" floor with their "clean" clothes. Isn't this after all what children do? They like to roll around on the floor. So scolding her husband about something as insignificant as laying their clothes on the floor was really unnecessary. It's virtually impossible to keep kid's clothes clean for an extended period of time.

But this wife was so consumed with having things her way, belittling her husband, brawling with him over insignificant things, and in a sense emasculating him by criticizing him in public, that she was unable to see the harm being done to her marriage. I'm almost certain that there were already fractures in their marriage that were more or less compounded by the stress of caring for eight children, and by the attention that the spotlight from the cameras garnered. All of this eventually led to the destruction of their marriage, and they divorced shortly after.

We will not always agree with everything our spouse does, but nevertheless, we should always respect them. Respect goes a long way in a marriage. Respect them for the uniqueness they bring to the table. Our spouse may not always do things the way we would do them; but so what. And who says that our way is the right way, anyway?

We have to release the need to try and control our spouse, or nag them into submitting to our will. This is never healthy in a marriage. These kind of marriages have a short lifespan, and usually only breed bitterness and ill-will, which is hard to overcome in a marriage.

Treat your spouse the way you would want to be treated. Better yet, treat him or her the way God tells us to treat our spouse in His word. God's way never fails; it will always be successful.

We must represent Christ, even in our marriage. This union was sanctioned by God and must, therefore, be kept holy. The church must set an example for the world to follow. They need to see, through us, God's design for marriage in its purest sense. Our marriage must be built upon God's principles, and be kept sacred, as God designed it to be. Marriage is a union best suited for mature, selfless individuals who are committed to each other, and who are willing to work tirelessly to create and maintain a well-balanced, Godly marriage. Build your marriage on biblical principles, and pray for God's grace to help you along the way.

THREE IS A CROWD

Marriage is a beautiful and sacred union that should be shared exclusively between two loving people. For this reason, you should never invite a third party into your marriage, either by revealing all of the intimate details of your marriage, or by inviting others to intimately participate in your marriage. By this, I am referring to the ungodly, unholy practices of "adultery" and "swinging."

Adultery is the voluntary sexual intercourse between a married person and someone other than their legal spouse. Swinging is the exchanging of spouses for sex. With swinging, both spouses are fully aware that their spouse is engaging in sex with another person. The swingers' lifestyle is accepted in certain circles.

Whether it's adultery or swinging, both can leave deep emotional scars in a marriage. When you become emotionally attached to someone other than your spouse, this causes fractures in your marriage. God does not want us to go outside of our marriage to find fulfillment. The fulfillment we seek should be found within the confounds of a loving marriage.

Trust is broken, sometimes irrevocably, by lies and deception. Adultery is lying to and deceiving your spouse about your love and fidelity. Jesus said that if you even look at a woman to lust after her, you have already committed adultery with her in your heart *(Matthew 5:27-28)*.

Adultery first starts in the heart, which, if left unchecked can often lead to the physical act of adultery. Once trust is broken in a marriage, you will never be able to fully trust your spouse again. Sure, you may be able to patch it up enough to allow yourselves to continue with the marriage, and you may even forgive, but you will never forget.

Resist the urge to stray outside of your marriage to find fulfillment. This is certainly not honoring God's command to love your spouse as you love yourself, giving of yourself sacrificially to them.

Choose to nurture the things that are healthy to a marriage: love, trust, fidelity, and mutual respect. The Christian marriage should be of the same pattern, and a true reflection of the holy communion between Christ and the Church. It should be built upon the foundation of love, and sacrificial in nature. Keep your marriage holy, which is most pleasing to God. The Bible provides us with all of the tools we need to create a holy and healthy union.

ONE BODY, ONE FLESH

There seem to be a lot of women who find pleasure in pushing their husbands away — of withholding intimacy. I'm not exactly sure why this is or even how it starts; but there seems to be some deep-seated resentment there. Maybe there were some issues early on in the marriage that were never dealt with. Maybe their husbands did or said something that offended them, but instead of bringing it to their husbands' attention, these women kept it buried inside, and have been holding it against him ever since.

Some marriages are only "surface marriages." They look good on the outside, but behind closed doors, the marriage is anything but perfect. More and more married people have their own lives apart from their spouse. He has his group of friends, and she has hers. Rarely do they come together as a couple, usually preferring to spend more time apart than they do together.

There's usually very little communication between these couples, other than when they discuss the children, or the household finances. They usually sleep separate from each other, with the husband sleeping in one part of the house, and the wife sleeping in another. But looking at it from the outside, you would never know. These couples have worked very hard over the years to conceal the true nature of their marriage. They have been able to hold the marriage together by a thin thread, trying to conceal, from the outside world, and their families, the fact that their marriage is no longer an emotional one, but one based on appearances alone. This is not healthy for a marriage.

Some women find their husbands to be selfish, thinking he cares more about himself than he does about his family. Some men have not mastered the art of showing their wives affection, or making her feel special. These men have probably been catered to their whole lives, or had mothers who did everything for them, and have, therefore, become accustomed to being the center of attention and never thinking about anyone other than themselves.

This type of personality never makes for a good husband. But clearly, these men have never had anyone to teach them how to be caring, loving, and supportive. Unfortunately, there are too many men like this out there who get into marriages with women who have high expectations for their marriage; but these men are never able to live up to any of these expectations.

Selfishness does not make for a good bedfellow. In

order for a marriage to be healthy, you must have two individuals who genuinely love each other, and are willing to give selflessly of themselves to make their marriage work.

You also need a certain level of maturity to make a marriage work. Immature people have no business getting married because marriage is not for the immature. These people need time to grow and to mature into their own before they even consider marriage.

Certain cultures believe in marrying their children off young. I think this has more to do with economics than anything. These families usually get a certain financial benefit from marrying off their young daughters. Often, these families are living in poverty, and find it difficult to put food on the table. They have developed certain cultural practices that they believe are essential for their survival.

But fortunately, we don't usually experience this type of desperation here in America. There are many wonderful programs that have been established to assist the poor. Our children in America can hope to get an education even if their parents can't afford to pay for it. No one has to go hungry here because there is always some sort of public assistance available, or a food pantry nearby which services the poor. We are truly blessed to live here in America.

Marriage is God's design, and His way of guaranteeing that no one is ever lonely, no one is ever without support, and that the earth is well-populated. God established this holy union for man's benefit. But man has begun to turn this sacred union into something that God never intended. As usual, man, in his desire to do things his own way, and because of his naturally disobedient heart, has taken God's sacred union and corrupted it. (Yep, I'm going there.) We have to talk about same-sex marriage. I know this is a taboo subject today, but God's word never changes; His word is still as relevant today as it was when He first gave it to His holy prophets to record in a book.

You often hear the question asked: "Where do you stand in the debate on same-sex marriage?" Well, I stand firmly behind God on this, which is where every

Christian should stand, not just on this topic, but on *all* topics. We should always stand in agreement with God. I would hate to be the one to try and go *against* God, on anything. It is to the believer's advantage to stand firmly behind the word of God, no matter how often society begins to shift and turn on certain issues.

God and His word is the one thing that will always remain the same. His word is a solid foundation; everything else is built upon sinking sand, and will one day crumble and fall. God's laws established the standard for marriage, and every believer must obey these laws. Even though society shifts and turns, all of God's laws remain unchangeable; God's laws will never change (period!). God is the same God, yesterday, today, and forever. We must obey God. He expects this of His children.

God's design for marriage is pure and holy; and it keeps corruption out. Because He is a holy God, He would never sanction anything that goes against His will, or leads us to sin against Him. Every time we sin against God, we spit in His face. Every time we disobey

Him, we step on His love. We have to ask ourselves, "what does God require of me?" Not, "what do I want to do?" In the end, the only thing that matters is what God thinks, not what you or I think or what society thinks, but what God thinks. He alone will stand in judgment of us.

God expects every believer to be holy. He expects us to obey Him, and to love Him as He loves us. We must also share this same love that God gives to us with the world. Freely we have received, and freely we must give. We are not called to be hateful and judgmental. We are to speak His word in love, considering that we were also once sinners in need of forgiveness for our sins. God's word is true, and we must stand firmly on it, not wavering or doubting.

You often hear Christians debate certain hot-button topics—such as same-sex marriage—with unbelievers. And surprisingly, these so-called Christians are almost spewing venom when they speak. The hatred for these particular groups is so clearly evident in these individuals. This is when you know that it's become personal with them. They are clearly approaching this from a holier-than-thou approach. We are to always walk in love, even when a person's behavior and/or lifestyle goes against God's laws. Our job is to stand up boldly and say, "Thus says the Lord." But we should not personally condemn these people. We have no heaven or hell to put anyone in. God will be the final judge of man; and if man is found to have obeyed God, and kept His commandments, he will be rewarded. But, if he has continuously and intentionally disobeyed God's commandments, he will be punished.

When the woman who was caught in the act of adultery was brought before Jesus, her accusers expected Him to condemn her to death. But Jesus did not condemn her; He forgave her, and told her to go and sin no more. We usually put all the emphasis on Jesus' pardon of her sin, but we cannot overlook what He told her after He had pardoned her: "go, and sin no more." When we are sincerely repentant, God will forgive us. But once we are forgiven, we are to continue in that forgiveness, and not go back into sin.

The Scripture is clear: "You shall not lie with a male as one lies with a female; it is an abomination" *(Leviticus 11:22)*. And, 1 Corinthians 6:9-10 says, "Or do you not know that the unrighteous will not inherit the kingdom of God? Do not be deceived; neither fornicators, nor idolaters, nor adulterers, nor effeminate, nor homosexuals, nor thieves, nor the covetous, nor drunkards, nor revilers, nor swindlers, will inherit the kingdom of God." What is there to debate? Christians should stand firmly behind the word of God, even if it makes you unpopular with the masses. The word of God has never been popular with the sinner; but whether it's popular or not, it is God's word.

We need to make sure we are keeping our marriage holy. We should not bring ungodly practices into our marriage. We must keep it holy. We should always honor our spouse, and respect them, not expecting anything of them that we ourselves are not willing and able to give. If you are willing to do the work, you can have a happy marriage that lasts for a lifetime. Talk out what is bothering you with your spouse. Don't let the sun go down on your wrath. Don't expect your spouse to be a mind reader; if something is bothering you, talk it out. Resolve all conflicts quickly, and quietly. Anything worth having is worth fighting for. And I strongly believe that a good marriage is worth fighting for.

קְדוּשָׁה
HOLINESS

Chapter 18

SEX AND DATING

I never really understood the whole premise of *dating without a purpose.* I've always considered dating to be a means to an end — the end being marriage. Personally, I don't even like to use the word *dating*; I think more along the lines of *courting*. Courting is something one engages in when he feels he is presently ready, and able, to settle down and get married. By now, he's thoroughly considered the qualities he wants in a wife, and believes he may have found someone who fits the bill. To get better acquainted with his intended, he begins to pursue her. And this is when the courting ritual begins.

Courtship was a term first used in the 16th century. It was the period when a man actively pursued a woman with expectations of *wooing* her, to win over her affections in order to seek a pledge of marriage.

> COURTSHIP WAS A TERM FIRST USED IN THE 16TH CENTURY.

The man, believing he can convince the woman to see him as a viable candidate, and to curry favor with her family, spends time with her and her family, impressing her with his wit, and flattering her with his charm. He may bring her flowers or a bottle of her favorite perfume. Or, he loads a picnic basket full of goodies, and chooses the perfect spot where the two of them enjoy a late afternoon lunch and picnic in the park. The happy couple even starts to open up and share with each other their dreams for the future. It's a time of pure bliss and innocence. There is no physical intimacy, as this is strictly forbidden and reserved for marriage. And if all goes well, they finally agree to a brief engagement, start making plans for their wedding, and eagerly anticipate a long life together with a house filled with children. I believe this sweet and innocent view of courting to be of the standard that God would approve.

In the early 1800s, young people were still expected to court with the intention of finding a life-long marriage partner. The word "date" was a phrase closely related to prostitution. It wasn't until the 1920s that dating for social reasons became a cultural phenomenon; even then, relationships were kept pure because premarital sex was still not accepted as the norm. (Wikipedia)

> THERE IS NO PHYSICAL INTIMACY, AS THIS IS STRICTLY FORBIDDEN AND RESERVED FOR MARRIAGE.

But dating has evolved to its more modern form of "hooking up" or "hanging out." Today, people seem to be only interested in having fun in the moment, coming together solely for the purpose of having a brief and casual sexual liaison. It is sometimes called "friends with benefits." There isn't much hope of these casual encounters ever leading to marriage. Sadly, it is quickly becoming commonplace for people to "hook up" with multiple partners, this being no longer frowned upon in society.

I strongly feel that "hooking up" and "hanging out" are not behaviors that God sanctions for Christians. Neither is premarital sex, for the Bible says that we are not to indulge in fornication because it defiles the body *(Matthew 15:19)*. Our bodies are the temples where God's Spirit resides; for this reason, we are to keep our temples clean and free from sin.

Every other sin that a man commits is outside of the body. But the man who commits fornication sins against his own body *(1 Corinthians 6:18)*. Because the Holy Ghost lives in us, we should glorify God with our bodies.

Abstaining from the things that defile us keeps us in right-standing with God. We undoubtedly grieve the

Holy Ghost when we invite sin and wickedness into our temples. We are to keep our bodies sacred and set aside for God's purpose and plan. Keeping sin outside of our members keeps God's light brightly burning within. Unquestionably, the modern dating culture is not in line with the spirit of holiness. It can lead to moral corruption, thereby bringing shame rather than glory to God.

One of the questions frequently asked by single Christians is: "Is it okay for Christians to date?" For this reason, we will take a look at whether the Christian, who routinely and habitually dates, is at risk of jeopardizing his or her good-standing with God.

The average long-term relationship could last anywhere from 18 months to 2 years. For an illustration, let's look at a person who starts dating at the age of 16 and continues to date up until age 21, when she finally marries. On average, she would have had 3 to 4 partners.

One question anyone who is seriously considering dating should ask himself/herself is: "Can I maintain a long-term relationship and keep it purely platonic—free from sensual desires?" Most relationships evolve over time. Naturally, as you spend more time with a person, your feelings for them become stronger. Stronger feelings usually lead to stronger sexual desires. The stronger and more forceful the sexual desires become, the harder it is to resist them. This is how people fall into sexual sin.

It is foolish for anyone to think that they are strong enough to be in a long-term relationship with someone for whom they have a strong physical attraction, and not be tempted to sin. You are inviting the temptation, making it virtually impossible to resist.

In the example above, the young lady has had roughly 3 to 4 dating partners. Everyone, by now, knows the evolution of most relationships, and how they can quickly escalate and get out of hand. In the beginning, the newly-minted couple hangs out together with a group of their friends. But as the relationship matures, they gradually break off from the group and start spending more time together alone.

The young man, because he is hormonal and

because he feels pressured by his peers to have sexual intercourse, starts pressuring her to have sex. At first she resists because she is not ready to take their relationship to the next level. But, as time goes on the guy becomes more relentless, reassuring her of his love and his desire to marry her one day. She loves him and doesn't want to lose him, and feels that if she doesn't have sex with him he may be tempted to find someone else who will. She is torn, and doesn't know what she should do. She consults with her girlfriends who tell her she should do it, and that it's no big deal. And, "girl, if you don't do it he'll just find someone who will." Under tremendous pressure, and out of a fear of losing him, she eventually gives in and has sex with him. After it is over, she feels a sense of great loss and regret.

Her regret in giving in to the pressure, and succumbing to the weakness of the flesh, leads to a feeling of guilt and shame. The guilt of sin riding high on her conscience causes a separation between herself and God, because how can she continue to feel close to God after she feels she's let Him down? Their once stable relationship is now in jeopardy.

Her church attendance starts to suffer because she feels as though everyone there is looking at her differently, and knows that she has sinned. Further still, she finds that once she's opened the door to sin, just like a dam break, the barrier has been broken allowing an easier access for more sin. She feels ashamed, and all alone. She's now drifting on a sea of guilt, unsure of how to stop the flow of the currents.

So you see, not having a true understanding of the doors we open when we adopt such a casual, worldly-view of dating can lead to serious problems in our relationship with God. It can cause a separation. The longer the door remains open, the problems continue to grow and escalate, pushing us further and further away from God.

When I was in Bible School, to receive practicum credit I attended a marriage seminar/workshop. The participants there where newly-engaged couples who were required to attend the seminar prior to getting married. There were two couples present at the session

I attended. I was mostly there as an observer, assisting the facilitator wherever I could. One couple in particular kept drawing the attention of my observant eye. I couldn't help but notice how extremely affectionate they were with each other. For most of the seminar this couple sat extremely close and kept up a perpetual marathon of hugging, caressing, and hand-holding. They couldn't seem to keep their hands off each other.

She seemed to me to be the bigger aggressor. For when he would appear to become lax in his caressing or attention, she would give him an ever-so-subtle signal: she would briefly touch his leg, or gently rub his hand, or she might scoot even closer to him (if this were possible!!), leaning her ample bosom even further into him. He would, of course, immediately pick up her signal and again continue his stream of affectionate rubbing and caressing. This would satisfy her for the moment, until he would once again become lax, to which she would then give him another subtle signal which he quickly intercepted and thus resume his caressing. This back and forth went on for the duration of the seminar.

If the facilitator noticed, she never said anything. But I couldn't help but notice. I guess I couldn't believe how people who profess to be Christians could be so comfortable interacting with one another as if they were already married. Looking at them in any other setting, you would naturally assume they were married. And one would only have to examine their body language, as I did, and assume they were probably already having sexual intercourse. They were just too familiar with each other not to be; and it would be almost impossible for them to convince me otherwise.

In holiness, there have to be certain barriers that we do not cross. God, in His infinite wisdom gave us His holy standards so that we wouldn't continue to behave like the world. He wants us to come out from among them and be separate. Different. A holy and a peculiar people, which is pleasing to Him.

God did not establish these standards to spoil our fun, as we might suppose. He established them because He knew that without them we would continue our sinful practices, thereby defiling ourselves over and over again. God knows that we would naturally want to continue living according to the standards that *we* feel are acceptable. Every person has a set of personal, moral codes that he or she tries to live by. But even in that, we must remember that our ways are still not compatible with God's ways. His ways are higher. Better. Stronger. More pure. In the end, we have to live by God's standards, not our own. God's standards are pure and holy. Our standards are self-serving and cater to the flesh.

The thing to understand about God's standards is that they are usually the total opposite of the world's standards. The world says, "you need to try it out first to see if you like it." And, "what if you get into a marriage and discover the sex isn't good?" But, what they won't tell you is that when two people who have kept themselves only for their spouse come together in pure, authentic love, the passion is so great between them that they have no desire for anyone else.

Not only do they not have a desire for anyone else, but their past relationships (because there are none) don't keep popping up and interfering with their present marriage. Nor do they have any active memories of past sexual partners knocking at the door of their hearts saying, "remember me?" while they are making love to their spouse. God's way eliminates all of the confusion and headache over having to manipulate our way through a jungle of past hurts, emotions, and the unhealthy soul-ties that we establish with multiple partners.

So, in my opinion, dating, or more preferably, courting, is something that should be entered into with the intent to marry. And it should be kept pure and holy. We should not allow ourselves to cross the boundaries God has established for us. Understand and accept that the flesh is weak; and if we do not control it, it will control us.

KEEPING SIN OUT

How do we control the flesh? First of all, by being alert to the things that we allow to enter into our bodies through our members. The things we take in through our eyes, ears, and minds can contaminate us.

What we watch on television can negatively influence our spiritual lives, and grieve the Holy Ghost. I'm noticing a trend in the quality of television shows today, or should I say, "lack of quality." Years ago, we had a more family-friendly lineup. Shows such as: *Andy Griffith, Little House on the Prairie, the Brady Bunch, and the Cosby Show*, topped the list. Today, we have *Revenge, Scandal, Desperate Housewives, and Modern Family* – the titles alone say it all. Television now appears to desecrate the family, rather than celebrate it.

We glorify violence, scandal, greed, lust, corruption, and sex. Feeding ourselves daily doses of this ungodly material only edifies and strengthens the flesh while diminishing the health and well-being of our spirit man.

I used to watch a certain television network (which shall remain nameless) that caters specifically to women. In fact, their tagline is: "Television for Women." I absolutely loved this network; I couldn't seem to get enough of it. I could always be certain to find a good movie playing whenever I turned to this channel. In fact, my weekends were usually consumed with watching back-to-back movie marathons on this channel. The movies were always riveting, filled with intrigue, and lots of drama. I became addicted right away.

Fortunately for me, one day, something clicked: the skies opened up, a flash bulb went off in my head, I received an awakening. It was equivalent to a bear waking up from a long hibernation, and suddenly becoming aware of her surroundings. I, at once, became aware for the first time of the type of material I was ingesting by watching the movies on this channel. From what I saw, a great majority of the movies mostly followed a certain theme: scandal, violence, sex, and betrayal.

The story lines predominantly revolved around: one woman sleeping with another woman's husband; a jealous lover exacting revenge on an unfaithful mate; a woman, unfulfilled in her marriage, seeks comfort in the arms of her husband's brother. On and on it went.

Because of this awakening, I could see for the first

time the seeds of corruption that were being planted in my spirit, and I was becoming desensitized to it. I knew I needed to immediately stop the influx of more corruption by discontinuing these movie marathon sessions. This sort of material was *not* edifying to my spirit. In fact, the longer I continued to take it in, the more corrupt I would become. So I stopped watching the channel altogether, and even deleted the channel from my television remote (to skip over it while channel surfing). But I didn't stop there. I eventually got rid of cable television altogether.

The days of pure, quality television programming are over. Although there are still a few good shows out there, the majority of them do nothing more than plant seeds of corruption, making it extremely difficult for us to walk in holiness. We need to be forceful about removing corruption from our hearts.

The eye is the lamp of the body. If our eye is clear, the whole body is full of light. But if the eye is bad, the whole body is full of darkness *(Matthew 6:22)*. When you view explicit and x-rated material, be it on television, the

Internet, or in books and magazines, you unconsciously fill the body with darkness.

Once you've been exposed, it's nearly impossible to erase the negative images from your mind; they are always there. You may find yourself replaying them over and over in your head, and fantasizing about them all day and night. Pretty soon, fantasy becomes reality when you begin to act them out.

It's not hard to see why Christians sometimes find it difficult to keep themselves pure and holy before God — free of impurities. They've been fed a steady diet of immorality, which feeds the flesh, making it stronger and more dominant over the spirit. The Apostle Paul admonishes us to present our bodies to God as a living, and holy sacrifice, which is acceptable to God, and our spiritual service of worship *(Romans 12:1)*.

It becomes difficult not to indulge in sexual sin when you watch it all day on television, or view it on the Internet, or fantasize about it in your dreams. If you see, hear, and meditate on something long enough, it becomes part of you.

The Christian must set a guard over his or her heart. We must guard ourselves from the things that lead to sin, and separation from God. Be willing to do whatever it takes to protect yourself, even if it means that you have to stop watching some of your favorite television shows. Set up filters on your computer(s) to block inappropriate content; or remove inappropriate channels from your cable television account. Whatever you need to do, do it!

If you are committed to living holy, as God requires all of us to do, you can do it. God is willing and able to help. Do not give in to every whim and craving of the flesh. Keep your body under subjection to the Spirit of God, and unspotted from the world. You should desire to grow and develop a meaningful and deep relationship with God, free of guilt, and be prepared to do the work to make this happen.

First, you must have an unwavering belief that holiness is God's will. He required it of Israel, and He requires it of us today. When you believe in something strong enough, you are willing to do whatever is necessary to achieve it. Your belief system must be based on biblical principles. Prayerfully ask God to help you, and to give you the strength to remain pure before Him.

Next, be assertive in limiting, and eventually closing and removing all avenues by which corruption seeps into your heart. Even if it means letting go of some friends, not watching certain things on television (sitcoms, commercials, etc.), banning perverted books and magazines from your home, and blocking explicit content on the Internet. Your active commitment to holiness is pleasing to God.

Third, seek to gain an understanding of how the flesh operates. Our flesh is an enemy of God. Even after we're saved, we will still continue to have problems in our flesh. The flesh is persistently wicked and full of corruption. Paul said, "in my flesh dwelleth no good thing" *(Romans 7:18).*

The world teaches us to pamper the flesh, and to do those things that are pleasing to the flesh. But the Bible tells us to crucify the flesh *(Galatians 5:24).* To kill something means you cut off its life supply — the thing that gives it life. We must begin to cut off the things that give the flesh its life-sustaining blood.

The flesh is built up and strengthened when, instead of reading the Holy Bible, we read romance novels. Or, when we listen to secular music, that glorifies sin, rather than pure worship music, that glorifies God.

Our flesh becomes weakened when we occasionally deny it nutrients through regular fasting. You'll find that when you begin to fast regularly those loud, ravenous cravings of the flesh are weakened and lose some of its forcefulness because you are crucifying the flesh while strengthening the spirit. So the spirit finally begins to dominate over the flesh, whereas before, the flesh was always doing the dominating. Crucifying the flesh is the best way to control it, allowing you a greater ability to live holy.

Finally, we need to keep our bodies, minds, and souls free from sin. A regular stream of fasting, praying, and reading the Bible strengthens and builds up our spiritual selves, while causing the fleshly side of us to become less dominant and easier to keep under the authority of

God. When we walk everyday according to the Spirit, we will not fulfill the lust of the flesh *(Galatians 5:16)*. When we run into challenges God is there to offer us the strength we need to make it through and to remain victorious over the flesh.

Keep your eyes and ears open, and be alert to your surroundings. Know the areas where you are the weakest and try and avoid them, whenever possible. Do not flirt with sin. Do not attempt to see how close you can get to sin without actually crossing over. Sin is sometimes like a magnet, drawing everything near it in with its magnetic fields. And once it snatches you up it can be difficult to free yourself.

So, stay as far away from sin as is humanly possible. Keep it out of your members. Do not entertain lustful thoughts. Do not indulge in sin, thinking you can ask for forgiveness afterward. Many people have tried, and some have actually died in their sins. There is no forgiveness in the grave for those who have died in sin. And tomorrow is not promised to any of us. So, *today* is the day to live holy for the Lord. He's calling us out of darkness into a life of holiness. Is anyone willing to answer the call?

קְדוּשָׁה
HOLINESS

Chapter 19

LETTER TO THE ROMAN CHURCH

The Apostle Paul, in his letter to the church in Rome, sought to encourage the church in their faith, and to provide further instructions to them on the message of grace, and faith in Jesus Christ, by which righteousness comes. Paul also wanted to show them what was expected of them as believers. He commended them for their faith, which was known worldwide, and wished to one day be able to see them in person in order to strengthen and encourage them personally.

The church at Rome appears to be composed mostly of Gentiles, with a few Jewish groups mixed in. Paul, being a Roman citizen, would certainly know the inner workings of the Roman mind-set, and also that of the Jewish sect of the Pharisees, to which he also belonged. He knew some of the challenges the church in Rome faced, and wrote this letter to encourage, motivate, and instruct them in their faith.

After his conversion, Paul spent three years in Nabatean Arabia, where he said he received his doctrine, as direct revelation from the Lord; the gospel that he preached did not come from man. It is this doctrine that he wanted to impart to the church in Rome, and to all the other individuals and churches he addressed in his many letters.

Paul wanted the believers in Rome to understand that they receive justification by faith (belief in, adherence to Christ), and not by works of the law. The law, said Paul, only points out your sins (flaws, failures, shortcomings), but it cannot save you. Your belief and complete trust in Jesus Christ is what saves you.

The Jews were naturally very religious, and were taught from birth to adhere to the law. But, the Scriptures really show us that it's impossible for a mortal man to abide by every law, which is why Jesus' death and resurrection is so important. His blood did what the law could not do—save us.

Paul says that in man's members (flesh) works all manner of sin and wickedness. Sin has taken over and now controls man, which leads to death and wrong-standing, or total separation from God. Without God's Holy Spirit in us, leading us and guiding us in the ways of righteousness, our sinful nature would continue to be the dominant force, causing us to walk in darkness. But the Holy Ghost leads us into the light.

In his letter to the church at Rome, Paul stressed the importance of faith; for it is our faith in God that makes us righteous, not our works. Therefore, it is important to sacrifice the sinful desires, and urges of the flesh, putting them to death so that God's Holy Spirit, which dwells in us, can lead us into righteousness (right-standing with God).

It's not the fact that some of the believers were Jews (the seed of Abraham, Isaac, and Jacob) that made them righteous. It is their complete trust and adherence to Jesus that makes them righteous. Thus, they were not to rely solely on their earthly lineage, and allow themselves to get puffed up with pride. But, they were to humble themselves, thereby making themselves pleasing to God.

PAUL'S LETTER TO THE ROMANS IS APPLICABLE TO THE CHURCH TODAY

Today, much like some of the Jews in the early church, some of us also tend to prefer a works-based salvation. We want our salvation to be contingent on the "good" that we do. Everyone usually thinks that he or she is a good person; and because of this, some think that it is their goodness that will secure them a place in heaven. But God's plan of salvation is not based on our standards; it is based on His.

Under our own standards, we would no doubt try and perform as many good deeds as we can in an attempt to try and purchase our salvation. This sort of thinking may lead us to believe that as long as our good deeds outweigh our bad then that makes us predominately good. But, it is by no goodness of our own that we are saved. It is the Lord that saved us when He purchased our salvation on the cross. There was no one else on earth who was found worthy to sacrifice his life for the sins of the world, so Jesus sacrificed His life instead.

Just as Jesus was crucified on the cross, we should all crucify our flesh daily, submitting ourselves to the leading of the Holy Ghost, just as Jesus submitted to death on the cross in order to purchase our salvation.

God requires us to "put off" the works of the flesh (malice, envy, greed, hatred, adultery, pride) and "put on" godliness (love, peace, joy, long-suffering, gentleness, humility) as a garment. We are, therefore, to robe ourselves in the righteousness of Christ, and to do away with the works of the flesh.

In the first chapter, verse 7, Paul told the church at Rome that they were called to be saints, and that they were designated for a consecrated life. This is true for us today. Our lives must be a sacrifice of all things that are pleasing to the flesh in order to walk in communion and fellowship with God.

Not only is the gospel the power of God working unto salvation, it also reveals a righteousness which God ascribes, which is disclosed through faith, and once revealed, leads to more faith. So, if you want to know what God requires of you, study the Bible, follow the leading of the Holy Ghost, and walk by faith.

Man, because of his sinful nature, for centuries has submitted to the lusts of the flesh; therefore, God gave them over and abandoned them to their vile and unnatural affections (that they practice in their members), which lead to death and God's righteous judgment.

The church should not think that it can judge and condemn those who practice sin, and yet practice these things themselves. Just because we are under grace does not mean that we will escape God's judgment if we continue to pursue and practice sin. God's kindness is given to us to lead us to repentance, not so that we can continue practicing sin.

Those who habitually do evil are storing up wrath, and God's judgment for themselves — and this includes the church. On the other hand, those who habitually do good shall receive glory, and honor, and peace.

HOLINESS

Chapter 20

LETTER TO THE THESSALONIAN CHURCH

While in Thessalonica, Paul spent three Sabbaths in the Jewish Synagogue expounding on the Scriptures and showing the Jews, through the Scriptures, that Jesus Christ was the Messiah. Some believed, along with a great number of Greeks, and a few leading women. But the unbelieving Jews, provoked by jealousy, stirred up a mob against Paul and Silas seeking to punish them for their doctrine. Because of the tumult and rowdiness of the crowds, Paul and Silas were eventually forced to leave.

Timothy, who later traveled back to Thessalonica, brought back to Paul a report about the conditions there. In Paul's letter to the Thessalonian church he commended them for their courage in times of persecution, for their complete trust and confidence in the Lord's power, and for how they eagerly await the coming of Jesus Christ.

Paul's letter is warm, friendly, and comforting. It is evident through his letter how much he truly loves this church, and has a great longing to see them again. His love for them is similar to the love of a father for his son. He speaks well of them, is encouraged by their unwavering faith in Jesus Christ, and really encourages them to continue in their faith and to anticipate the coming of Jesus, when He will rescue them, and us, from further persecutions and hardships.

He reminds the saints at Thessalonica of God's

will for them: to walk and live holy; to abstain from all sexual vice, learning how to possess (control) their own bodies in consecration (purity) and honor; to not be like the heathens, who are ignorant of God and who submit to the passion of their lusts; and finally, to not transgress their brother or defraud him in business matters.

Paul tells them that God is an avenger of such transgressions of the law. And the apostles have already warned us against such things. God has called us to purity, and whoever disregards or rejects this is not rejecting man, but is rejecting God. The Spirit that God gives to us is holy, so we must likewise be holy.

Paul admonishes the church to excel more and more in love one for another, to live quiet and peacefully minding their own affairs, and to work with their hands, not being a burden to others.

Paul goes on to say: there's also something you must know about those who have fallen asleep (in death). You must not grieve as those who have no hope. We have hope beyond the grave, in Jesus Christ, who Himself died and rose to life again, and will bring with Him those who have fallen asleep when He returns.

Those who are alive at the coming of Jesus will have no advantage over those who have fallen asleep in death. For the Lord will descend from heaven with a shout, and a blast of the trumpet of God, and those who are asleep in Christ will rise first, then we which are living shall simultaneously be caught up together with the resurrected ones in the clouds to meet the Lord in the air, and will always be with the Lord. Therefore, comfort and encourage one another with these words.

As to the precise time this event will occur, you need not know, for you yourselves know perfectly well that the day of the Lord's return will come suddenly, as a thief in the night. But you are not in darkness that this day will overtake you by surprise like a thief, for you are sons of light, and the day, and do not belong to the darkness.

Accordingly, keep wide awake and alert; be watchful and cautious. God has not appointed us to incur His wrath, but that we might obtain His salvation through Jesus Christ, the Messiah, who died for us so that whether we are still alive or dead at Christ's appearing, we might live together with Him, and share His life.

Therefore, encourage one another, and strengthen and build up one another, be unceasing in prayer, and thank God in everything, no matter what the circumstances may be.

PAUL'S LETTER TO THE THESSALONIANS IS APPLICABLE TO THE CHURCH TODAY

We have a Father who loves us, and thinks highly of us. He rewards us when we are good and obedient children, and chastises us when we go astray. God's goal is to perfect us in holiness, making us more like Him. His desire for us is that we be ready to meet the Lord in the air when the trumpet sounds, and when the archangel shouts, calling His people home to their final resting place.

But, if we are distracted, asleep, or have fallen away when Jesus returns suddenly for His church, we could very well miss this opportunity to return with Jesus, and have to endure much tribulation, which we have not been destined for. The *tribulation* is for the disobedient and the ungodly — those who have rejected God's laws, and His offer of salvation through Jesus Christ. God will pour out His wrath on the earth and defeat all the enemies of God, wiping sin from the earth and restoring it back to its original sinless state, as it was before the fall.

Paul told the Thessalonians how to please God in sanctification: by remaining pure and holy before God; not giving in to the lusts of the flesh; not defiling their bodies with sexual sins; and by not dealing unethically with their brothers. But they were to love one another, and be affectionate and kind to one another. This is sanctification; and it pleases God.

The church today must also seek to please God, obey all of His commands, and honor Him body, mind, and spirit. We must learn to live together in unity, having one mind, and anxiously await Jesus' return.

We should also be steadfast in our faith, even through persecution. Here in America, the church is not often in fear for their lives as some Christians in other countries are. But, we still need to be bold and uncompromising in our faith, and in the doctrine which we have been given.

Today, the enemies of God are trying to silence and intimidate the church. The world doesn't want to hear that they are in sin, and that they must repent and turn away from sin or suffer God's wrath. They have fought against public prayers, and any kind of religious expression in public.

These people seek to silence the church on topics such as homosexuality, adultery, fornication, greed, and pride. They threaten the church with lawsuits, and with the removal of their tax-exempt status if the church continues to preach the gospel, which they call "spreading hate and intolerance." But what these people do not realize is that you cannot stop the gospel from being preached. Because, if you are successful in intimidating one or two wavering Christians, there are many more who are bold and unafraid, and will not be intimidated, but are determined to preach the gospel until Christ returns.

The gospel is God's holy word for mankind; and His word will continue to be preached on the earth, even if He has to raise up a few stones to do so, or speak through a donkey. You cannot stop God! The world will be judged out of the things that are written in the Holy Bible, and will one day have to answer to God for their sins. So, thinking you can escape God's righteous judgment by shutting up His saints is useless, and will never work.

The church must be bold and courageous for God. The saints in Thessalonica faced enormous persecution by those unbelieving Jews who sought to discredit them, and to stop the gospel from spreading. But, as we see in Paul's letter, the church stood up under the persecution, and their faith in God the Father and Jesus Christ the Messiah was stronger than ever.

Therefore, like the Thessalonians, we must continue to spread the gospel, in love, knowing that the day will come when Jesus Christ will rescue us from our persecutions and hardships. He will avenge His own, and His name will forever be proclaimed on the earth.

When Christ returns for His church, make sure you are prepared to answer the call when He summons us home. Keep your garments unspotted from sin. Remain holy and perfect (mature) before God. Love one another. Show Christian unity. And be on guard, waiting patiently for His return.

HOLINESS

Chapter 21

LETTER TO THE CORINTHIAN CHURCH

Paul spent a year and a half in Corinth, establishing the church there. And as was his custom, every Sabbath he would enter the Jewish Synagogue and reason with them regarding Jesus Christ—that He was the Messiah. Some Jews believed, and others did not.

While at Corinth, Paul met a Jew named Aquila,

and his wife Priscilla. They were noble Jews who happened to have had the same occupation as Paul—they were tentmakers. While in Corinth, Paul stayed with Aquila and Priscilla; and in addition to preaching in the Synagogue every Sabbath, he worked with them making tents.

Many of the Corinthians heard the gospel message and believed, and were baptized. But some were jealous of Paul, and rejected his message, causing an insurrection among the Jews, bringing Paul before the courts to answer to charges that he was teaching men to worship God contrary to the law. But the judge would not even hear these accusers, not willing to judge matters relating to Jewish law; so, he drove them from the courts encouraging them to settle the matter among themselves. Shortly after, Paul left Corinth, sailing to Syria and coming to Ephesus.

Although Paul had made a few enemies during his time in Corinth, he also established quite a few lasting friendships. So, I can imagine the church's excitement when they received his letter, in which he addressed many things — some of which we will discuss here.

Paul wrote about the need for unity. He told the church that there should be no divisions or factions in the church, and that they should all speak the same things, and be perfectly joined together in the same mind.

Some in the church were apparently quarreling among themselves, with some saying, I am of Paul, and others saying, I am of Apollos, and others still, I am of Cephas (Peter), while some claimed to be of Christ. They had broken off into small groups, creating warring sects of believers. But Paul warned them against this, saying that we are all members of the same body, with Jesus Christ as the head. The apostles are just special messengers who God used to preach the gospel; but the gospel is of God, not of man.

Paul also compared and contrasted the wisdom of God with the wisdom of the world. The wisdom of God, he said, is considered foolishness to the world because they are not saved. We can never understand God through our human intellect because our human intellect is not able to comprehend a great God. God chose the lesser things to confound the wise. In their human wisdom, they (those following after worldly wisdom) are not able to comprehend even small things. Their wisdom has blinded them. Even what seems foolish in God is wiser than man; and the weakness of God is stronger than man.

Paul also briefly addressed the Spirit of God. He told the Corinthian church that he did not come to them as an orator, with a display of showy words that showcased his vocal skills and abilities, but he came to them in demonstration of the Spirit and power of God, which showcased God's power.

He goes on to say that we speak the wisdom of God in a mystery, which is revealed to us by God's own Spirit. For what man knows the mind of man, except his own spirit which is inside of him? Likewise, no one knows or understands the mind of God, except His own Spirit.

God has revealed His will and His way to us through His Spirit, which now resides in the Spirit-filled believer.

The Spirit searches the deep things of God, and reveals them to us. This is why it is important that we are filled with His Spirit. It is His Spirit that leads us into all truth.

Paul also addressed fornication and the need for purity. He had heard rumors that there was fornication among the believers in the Corinthian church, namely, one who had slept with his father's wife. He told them that this is behavior that should never take place among those who are saved. This is something that is common among the heathens, not among the saints. Nor should you tolerate such behavior, but put the offender out before this corrupt behavior spreads throughout the church. For when we tolerate such behavior, it invariably infects the whole church. We must, therefore, address it immediately to prevent it from spreading further.

Fornication is sin. Every other sin that a man does is outside of the body, but the one who commits fornication sins against his own body. We should, therefore, keep sin out of our bodies because our bodies are the temples where God's Spirit dwells; therefore, our bodies are to be kept holy. We should glorify God in our bodies, for we now belong to Him.

Paul goes on to say that we must always remember those who have gone before us. Remember how Israel's disobedience in the wilderness stirred up God's wrath. Their hearts were evil; they refused to obey Him; and because of this, many of them died in the wilderness. They were idolaters, fornicators, they tempted God, and they murmured and complained against Him. These things were done for our example. They show us how we should not behave. If we obey God and keep His commandments, we will inherit the blessings. But if we refuse to heed His voice, we will bring upon ourselves God's holy wrath.

We should all be followers of Christ, as He is the head of the church. Everyone should reverence his head, not bringing shame to the body of Christ.

Paul also wrote to the Corinthians about spiritual gifts. These gifts, he said, come from God. And although there is a diversity of gifts and administrations, they are all from the same Spirit—God's Holy Spirit. These gifts (word of wisdom, word of knowledge, faith, healing, miracles, prophecy, discerning of spirits, tongues, and interpretation of tongues) are given to you for the edification of the church. They are to be used to help strengthen and establish the church.

Therefore, desire the best gifts, and use them wisely. Also, humble yourselves before God, and do not seek to bring attention to yourselves. Use the gifts that have been given you to benefit the church, and for the furtherance of the gospel.

Paul's letter also addressed false teachings in the church. Some men were saying that Christ did not rise from the dead. But Paul told them that there was proof that Jesus did in fact rise from the grave after three days; for He was seen of numerous witnesses who all testify to the fact that He is risen. Paul reminded the saints that their faith was built upon Christ's resurrection from the dead; and if He were not alive, their faith would then be in vain.

Christ is the first-fruits of those who have died. There will come a resurrection of the dead where we will no longer be housed in a temporary, corruptible body. There is a natural body, and there is a spiritual body. We are all housed in an earthly body, which will one day become spiritual bodies, which are not made of corruptible flesh; our new spiritual bodies will be incorruptible. We will also be changed, in a moment in the twinkling of an eye, and the dead in Christ will be raised to a new eternal life in Christ, just as Christ was risen from the grave to a new life, where He is now seated at the right hand of God.

Finally, Paul admonished the church to remain steadfast, unmovable, always abounding in the work of the Lord, because their labor is not in vain.

PAUL'S LETTER TO THE CORINTHIANS IS APPLICABLE TO THE CHURCH TODAY

Just as there was a need for unity among the saints in the Corinthian church, there is also a need for unity among the church today. We serve one God, and there is one Holy Bible, which teaches us the ways of God, and shows us how to please Him. But somehow we've broken our unity and veered away from our common faith. The church has split and gone in different directions. We do not all speak the same thing or believe the same thing, which has created a separation among the people of God.

There is reported to be approximately 41,000 different Christian denominations worldwide. (Wikipedia) They all confess faith in God, and in the Bible as His holy word. But, unfortunately, each denomination has their own separate doctrine, which is based on their own interpretation of Scripture.

It's highly likely that many of these Christian denominations were formed because of a split in the church, possibly due to a disagreement regarding their interpretation of Scripture, or a disagreement as to who should be the leader (or pastor) of the church. And, when they could not come to an agreement, someone decided to break away and start his or her own church, or a new denomination, usually with himself or herself as the leader. This, unfortunately, is often how many of these denominations are started.

God did not call us to build competing denominations. He left His church in our hands, instructing us to build it up and to preach the gospel throughout the entire world. God's church is not divided; it is a church united under Jesus Christ, with Him as its God-appointed leader. He alone gave His life for the church, making Him the only one worthy of being its leader. Jesus' shed blood at Calvary is what established the church. He shows us how to be servants of the kingdom, building up the church of God in unity and love.

We also need to beware of intellectualism, which comes from a natural, earthly perspective. This way of viewing things—through the human intellect—often competes with the spiritual aspects of the kingdom of God. God's kingdom is spiritual and not of this world, therefore, it is not built upon human philosophy and wisdom.

Human philosophy and wisdom are limited to what we can see, hear, and touch. If it can't be explained with our intellects then it must not exist. If we can't see it, touch it, or conceptualize it, then it can't be real.

God is a Spirit, and has no beginning or end. He transcends all time and space. Unlike man, God can be in more than one place at a time because He is a Spirit, and is not limited to a physical body as we are. God created the universe out of nothing by speaking it into existence. He formed man out of the dust of the ground, and breathed into his nostrils the breath of life. He pours out His Spirit upon man, and dwells in him, leading and directing him in the ways of God. This is not something that can be easily comprehended by natural man, with our human intellects. This all makes no sense to a natural man who believes that everything has to have a beginning and an end; and that if we can't see it, hear it, or touch it, it does not exist. We want physical proof before we believe. Without that proof, we find it difficult to believe.

Our belief in God must come through faith. Faith is spiritual, not natural. Faith operates in the spiritual realm, not out of the natural realm. The natural realm is limited, but there are no limitations in the spiritual realm. Faith, therefore, is supernatural, meaning it surpasses the natural. This is why simply having faith creates the impossible in our lives. Because, when we operate out of faith, we are showing that we believe that the things we hope for *are* possible, even though human wisdom and logic tells us they are not possible. Through faith, we are proving that we believe God is far superior than man, and that there are no limitations in Him; therefore, we believe that He is able to create something out of nothing. We believe that God can make a way when there appears to be no way. And we simply believe that He is able to make the impossible, possible. This is why we should not put our trust in human wisdom, because it is fallible. Our belief should be in the wisdom and the power of God, which is far superior.

Finally, the Bible tells us to flee fornication. Paul addressed it in his letter to the Corinthian church, and we must address it in the church today. Fornication is sex outside of marriage. The Bible tells us to abstain from sexual relations if we are not married. When we fornicate, we sin against God by disobeying His commandments to not engage in sin. Disobeying God leads to His disapproval, and eventually to His wrath. God's wrath poured out is brutal. It is designed to punish the offender. May we always obey God, and pray for His mercy.

We defile our temples when we commit fornication. God's Holy Spirit cannot dwell in an unclean temple. Present your bodies to God as a holy and sacred place, which is pleasing and acceptable to God.

Submit to God, and allow Him to take care of the rest.

SECTION 3

FAITH

Chapter 22

WHAT IS FAITH?

So, what is faith? Think of it this way: Faith is something that happens outside a world where there are limits, barriers, conformity, and status quo. Faith operates in the sphere of what we would normally call "impossible." But in the faith world, there are no impossibilities. Nothing is impossible to you through faith.

In our current world, there are laws of gravity, time and space, barriers, and limitations. What we see is real. If we can't see it, hear it, touch it, or smell it, it doesn't exist. If we can understand it with our natural minds, or conceptualize it, then it is a part of our reality. Anything that *cannot* be understood with the human mind does not have a place in our world. This visible, audible, tangible, sensory realm is what we call the natural realm. This is where we live everyday, following along with all the rules and laws that govern this realm.

Faith is not a part of the natural realm. Faith operates in the supernatural realm. The supernatural realm is where God operates, along with all of His supernatural power. His power has no limitations or barriers. God's power does not conform to the rules and the laws of the natural realm. In fact, when God speaks to the natural elements, and our natural reality, they have to obey His voice. They bow to Him, and obey His every command. When God speaks, the barrier that exists between the natural and the supernatural realm is broken, making miracles possible. And what we call a miracle (a supernatural occurrence) in the natural realm, isn't a miracle at all in the supernatural realm; it's a normal everyday occurrence. God can penetrate the natural realm with His supernatural power to make miracles happen. Likewise, when our faith crashes through the barrier of the natural realm (this barrier that exists in our minds), and reaches into the supernatural realm, touching God's power, a miracle happens because it's our faith that activates God's power on earth, and it becomes visible for all to see.

> WE ARE SPIRITUAL BEINGS HOUSED IN A NATURAL BODY.

Faith is belief in the Lord God, His existence, His limitless power, and His ability and willingness to perform miracles in our lives. Faith believes that God is who He says He is, and that He can do what He says He can do. Faith pushes past the barriers that have been set up in our minds—which have been programmed to believe only the things we can see. We are spiritual beings housed in a natural body. Our natural bodies place limits on us, but our spirit beings know no such limits. So, if we can conquer, or overrule the flesh, our spirit can then penetrate the faith realm and activate, or connect with, God's supernatural powers.

This is why it is hard for some to believe in God. God is a Spirit; and it is hard for natural man to comprehend a spirit being because we cannot see Him with our natural eyes or touch Him. So, to our natural senses, if we can't see God or touch Him, He doesn't exist. But God *can* be perceived, or seen, with our spirit, through faith. We can see God, touch Him, and hear Him through the eyes of faith. God makes Himself clearly evident in our hearts, but some simply refuse to accept the things they know to be true in their hearts. They push away the faith that they have in their hearts, and cling to the natural man, who is a natural enemy of God.

I often hear people say that they don't believe in God. I just don't believe this is possible because it's *in us* to believe. Instead, these people *choose* not to believe, or deny what they know to be true in their hearts. And if you deny something long enough it becomes your reality and, thus, harder for you to believe.

Faith is the thing that most pleases God. For without faith it is impossible to please Him. Without faith, we are relegated to the natural realm where nothing of an extraordinary nature occurs. No miracles are expected in the natural realm because we know man's power is limited, and we have been wired to operate within this reality. But faith takes us out of our reality, and into God's reality, where there truly are no limits or impossibilities.

Faith operates in God's world, where there is freedom from doubt, fear, barriers, and limitations. Our faith takes us out of the impossible, to a place where everything is possible to the one who believes. When we walk in faith, our natural, ordinary minds are stripped of their debilitating control over us, and we are free to walk in the liberty of the extraordinary, nothing-is-impossible-through-faith minds that God desires us to have. Faith takes us from being controlled by the natural, to being empowered by the supernatural. When we walk in the power of the supernatural, God's power is manifested through us.

אֱמוּנָה
FAITH

Chapter 23

BARRIERS TO FAITH

LIFE EXPERIENCES

When I was a child — I was probably around four years old at the time — our teachers read to our Pre-k class the story of the *Gingerbread Man*. In the story, there was a little old man, and a little old woman, who lived alone in a little old cottage. They were both hungry, so the little old woman decided to make a gingerbread man cookie for them to eat. She made the gingerbread dough, rolled it out, and cut out the gingerbread man. After giving him two eyes, a nose, a mouth, and buttons down his chest, she placed him in the oven to bake. When the little old woman went to check on him, as soon as she opened the oven door, the gingerbread man stood up, leaped out of the oven, and ran across the room and out the door. She yelled at him to stop, but the gingerbread man kept running and shouting, "run, run, as fast as you can, you can't catch me I'm the gingerbread man!"

The little old man saw what was happening and began to chase after the gingerbread man, along with the little old woman. But he was too fast for them. He just kept running and shouting, "run, run, as fast as you can, you can't catch me I'm the gingerbread man!" In all, the gingerbread man ran past a cow, a horse, and a pig. They all yelled at him to stop, but he wouldn't, he kept running and taunting them, "run, run, as fast as you can, you can't catch me I'm the gingerbread man!" Soon, the gingerbread man came upon a fox. He told the fox how he had just outrun a little old woman, a little old man, a cow, a horse, and a pig, and he could outrun the fox too. But the fox feigned indifference; *he* was not interested in a gingerbread man, or so he pretended. So, the gingerbread man stopped running and decided to rest. As he was talking to the fox, the fox opened his mouth and clamped down on the gingerbread man. And that, was the end of the gingerbread man.

Shortly after we heard this story, our teachers told our class that we were going to take a "trip" down to the cafeteria. They told us there was a surprise awaiting us there. As you might imagine, we were all very excited. We loved an adventure, and could hardly contain our excitement. Soon, we were all lined up single file and proceeded to make our way to the cafeteria.

When we walked through the doors of the cafeteria, there, to our utter amazement, sitting on a sheet tray, was the most beautiful gingerbread man cookie we had ever seen. He had a beautiful brown hue, bright red buttons running down his chest, a twinkle in his eye, and a smile that appeared to light up the room. He was truly a sight to behold. And the aroma coming from this fresh-baked cookie was intoxicating. We were told the gingerbread man had just come out of the oven and needed to cool. But once he was cool enough to eat, we would all get to taste him. In the meantime, we headed back to our classroom to resume our day, but would only have a short wait until our beautiful gingerbread cookie was ready to eat. But for a group of excited four year olds, a few minutes felt like an eternity.

But finally, the time did arrive for us to make our way back to the cafeteria. We were overjoyed and could hardly contain our excitement as we eagerly anticipated the moment we would be able to sink our teeth into the ooey-gooey deliciousness of this fresh-baked gingerbread cookie. But when we walked into the cafeteria, there, to our complete horror and disbelief sat the sheet tray—which had previously held the gingerbread man cookie—now empty. We couldn't believe our eyes.

We were told that shortly after we left, one of the cafeteria workers went to check on him, and to her surprise, discovered he was gone. She looked all over for him but couldn't find him anywhere. Several more people joined in the search, but it was hopeless, he was nowhere to be found. They began to speculate that he, like the gingerbread man in the story, must have run away. Our four-year-old minds didn't know what to make of all this. Does this mean we *won't* get to eat the gingerbread cookie after all? We were all devastated by this new turn of events. How could this be? Why would he just run off? And how could this happen and no one notice?

> OUR FOUR-YEAR-OLD MINDS DIDN'T KNOW WHAT TO MAKE OF ALL THIS.

Sometime later, when I was older, something happened to trigger my memory of this day and the "runaway" gingerbread man. And as I was now much older and able to reflect on it with a more mature mind, I realized this story couldn't possibly be true; for it's just not possible for a cookie to, first of all, get up from a sheet tray, and then run away. This just didn't happen. It became clear to me then that our teachers had made it all up. They must have thought, given the fact we had just finished reading the story of the *Gingerbread Man*, that it would be fun to stage a "runaway" gingerbread man for us. To this day, it still amazes me that we were all too naive and gullible to see what was really going on. At the time, there was no doubt in our minds as to the validity of this story. But looking back on it now, I see that we were all young and impressionable and ready to believe anything an adult told us. Again, I'm sure it all seemed like harmless fun to them, but it amazes me that they thought it was okay to *lie* to a group of four year olds. And that's exactly what it was, a lie. Not a half-truth, or a "little white lie." It was a lie. We have a tendency to justify our lies by classifying them into categories. Somehow we think that "little white lies" are okay. But a lie, no matter how you look at it, is still a lie.

Needless to say, this lie hurt. The revelation of it cut through me like a knife. I felt a little betrayed by people I had trusted and looked up to. At one point, I even wanted to be a teacher. But maybe, what really hurt the most was knowing that I, with my little child's innocence, was unable to comprehend what was really going on at the time. I simply took their word for it. I was vulnerable; and that's never a good place to be.

But children *are* vulnerable. That's why we need to protect them and be careful what we say to them. You never know whether something you perceive to be harmless will scar a child for life. We must understand that the very thing we consider harmless or innocent, to a child, could feel like a betrayal. Children are innocent, and trusting. I was innocent; but this seemingly harmless lie began to cut away at my innocence like a serrated knife sawing through a loaf of fresh-baked bread.

The more lies we expose our children to (e.g. The Tooth Fairy, Santa Clause, The Gingerbread Man), the more we begin to cut away at their innocence. It is in essence like exposing a sweet innocent soul to a world of darkness and deceit for the first time. A lie, as harmless as we might mean it to be, can have a great and lasting impact on an impressionable child. It can reach down into a child's soul affecting him or her, and exposing this child to something that he or she has never been exposed to before—the dark world of lies and deception. So we have to always be mindful that we are not destroying a child's innocence with lies.

This is also the case for much of life's traumatic experiences. When a person is victimized, or experiences a significant amount of trauma, they are naturally affected. When a child experiences trauma, he or she can be deeply, and in some cases, irrevocably damaged. It's these experiences that then begin to shape who we are, and how we see the world. They can also begin to slowly chip away at the innocent world we've only ever known. Who we are is determined by our life experiences. And it's those early experiences that help set the stage for who we will become.

When a baby first emerges from the womb, she has no awareness of good or evil. She knows nothing of life's disappointments, sorrows, or pains. Babies are pure and innocent. In this stage of life, a baby is only able to view the world through the eyes of a pure heart. This is her only frame of reference, as she has not yet been tainted or soiled by the world.

That's why it is easy for a child to have child-like faith, because their perspective is still pure and innocent, and untainted. Their imaginations are ever-active and free-flowing. They can dream big dreams, and imagine themselves as kings and princesses who are able to slay the dragon. In their minds, anything they can think of is possible. That's faith. If you can see it and believe it, you can have it, be it, or achieve it. But unfortunately, the older children become, and the more experiences they have, it becomes harder for them to visualize and dream impossible dreams, like they did when they were younger. Others also begin to tell them that what they perceive to be real, is not real; that it's just make-believe; that none of it can actually happen.

How many times have we said this to our children? We are killing that innocent spark that God placed in them from birth, and taking away their ability to have pure faith. Our words are starting to change their perspective. That once pure and innocent mind is slowly being changed and reconditioned to view the world differently. They are being stripped of their innocence, which is now becoming tainted and soiled.

Faith is being able to see God through pure and innocent eyes that have not been tainted by the world. Faith is the *substance* of things hoped for, the *evidence* of things not seen *(Hebrews 11:1)*. It is being able to believe the things you do not see, and assured, or confident, of the things you cannot touch. You believe these things as though they are real and tangible. And once you believe something long enough, it becomes real to you. That is when that once impossible thing, that once invisible thing, becomes tangible, or attainable.

Faith draws things to you. Faith makes them real. If you believe God can heal you, even though the doctor says there is no hope, and you begin to visualize and see yourself healed, to the point where it becomes a reality in your spirit, you will be healed. The Lord responds to your faith. Faith is a *knowing* in your spirit that that impossible thing is possible with God.

Blind Bartimaeus sat by the side of the highway begging. When he heard that Jesus was passing by, he called out to Him. Jesus stopped and asked Bartimaeus, "what is it you want me to do for you?" Bartimaeus said, "Lord, I want to receive my sight." Jesus said to him, "go your way, your faith has made you whole." And immediately, Bartimaeus received his sight *(Mark 10:46-52)*. Bartimaeus did not let the crowd stop him. They tried to stop him from getting to Jesus. They tried to quiet him. But he was not deterred by the crowd. He needed something from the Lord. He wanted to receive his sight. Bartimaeus believed Jesus could heal him, therefore, he reached out to Jesus for healing, and received it. He believed that Jesus could do the impossible; that's when that once impossible situation became a reality, because he went away seeing.

What do you need from the Lord? Have you always seen it as impossible? Nothing is impossible with the Lord *(Luke 1:37)*. Call out to Him today, just like Bartimaeus did. Call out to Him in faith, believing that you will receive what you hope for. Believe Him to do the impossible in your life. Have faith in God.

LOGICAL THINKING

We are taught to think logically. If A, then B. If A happens, then B will happen next. In logical thinking, A is some variable that must occur before B can take place. Our parents at times may have told us: if you eat your vegetables, then you will grow big and strong. In other words, if you want to be big and strong, you must first eat your vegetables. When thinking logically, A must always take place first before B can occur.

We are taught that there is a natural order in nature. For example, first winter, then spring, then summer and fall. No one expects spring to come before winter. Winter must occur first, then spring. That's just the natural order of things. This is how God set things in order. We are logical beings who always expect things to happen a certain way; that is how we have been wired. We are programmed to think this way.

Logical thinking is a barrier to faith. In order to have faith, we must completely change our way of thinking. The thought patterns which have become so natural to us must be completely discarded in order for faith to take hold. It requires a complete overhaul of our mind.

This is where the Holy Ghost comes in. The Holy Ghost is the Spirit of God, which comes to dwell in a believer. The Bible says that God is a Spirit *(John 4:24)*. God is a spiritual being who pours out of Himself into the spirit of a believer, and infuses him or her with His essence (nature). Once we have been filled up with God, we are then able to think like God thinks because we have His Spirit residing in us, allowing us to tap into the mind and the thoughts of God. The Bible says, no man knows the thoughts of a man except the spirit of the man which is in him.

"But just as it is written,

"Things which eye has not seen and

ear has not heard, and which have

not entered the heart of man,

all that God has prepared for those who love Him."

For to us God revealed them through the Spirit;

for the Spirit searches all things,

even the depths of God.

For who among men knows the thoughts

> of a man except the spirit
> of the man which is in him?
> Even so the thoughts of God
> no one knows except the Spirit of God.
> Now we have received,
> not the spirit of the world,
> but the Spirit who is from God,
> so that we may know
> the things freely given to us by God."
> (1 Corinthians 2:9-12; emphasis added)

The Holy Ghost, which is the Spirit of God in us, searches the mind of God and reveals His thoughts to us. We are then able to understand the mind and the heart of God. We are able to think like He thinks and even do the things He does, because we are empowered by the Holy Ghost, which lives in us. We, therefore, have the ability to overcome the mind-set of the world. We are able to rise above its limitations, and see ourselves as God sees us. How does God see us? The Bible says, He sees us healed, delivered, victorious, and as overcomers. But, we must first overcome our worldly way of thinking, and being, in this world.

Before we were born-again, we thought like the world, and behaved according to worldly standards. We were not able to understand the things of God because we were not yet born of God; we were still born of the world. It's similar to an indoctrination. I once heard someone liken the period between natural birth and the "new birth" experience (when we become born-again believers), to going through training at the "University of Satan" (the *U of S*). The curriculum taught at the *U of S* sets us on a sure course for destruction.

The *U of S* is structured in a way that goes against the word and the will of God. There is a culture of disobedience that has been established there. This culture of disobedience teaches us to lie and to be deceptive, and to cheat and to try and get away with it. We are taught to put our own will and desires above God's. We begin to become boastful, and filled with pride. We start to hate the things of God, and love the things of the world. But all that is in the world is the lust of the flesh, the lust of the eye, and the pride of life *(1 John 2:16)*. These things are not of the Lord, but of the world. At the *U of S,* we are encouraged to pursue these things because we think they will make us happy. This indoctrination we go through, prior to salvation, must be removed from us by the Holy Ghost. It is a hindrance to faith.

And this is how we must see it, as an obstacle to our faith, and we must renew our minds daily in the word of God, not being conformed again to the patterns of this world. We must be transformed, for we are now new creatures; the old patterns and habits we once had have been washed away. We have been washed in the blood of the lamb. We must learn to walk daily in the new life God has given us through Jesus Christ.

Faith requires that we no longer think as the world thinks, but that we begin to think the way God thinks. We must rise above the physical and mental limitations we were once bound by in the world, because once we are born-again, we are no longer bound by these limitations.

Because God is a spiritual being, He is not restricted by the physical barriers of this world. Nor is God limited to time and space. He transcends time and space. While God can be present in the United States and Africa at the same time, we can only physically be in one place at a time. Because we are housed in a physical body, we are physically limited to time and space. In our earthly bodies, we are bound by the *laws of gravity,* and the *laws of physics*. We are also bound by time; but God is not. "One day is like a thousand years with the Lord" *(2 Peter 3:8)*.

But there is a way we can transcend above these physical limitations—through faith. Faith is like a seed that gets planted in the ground. When you begin to nourish and cultivate that seed, it starts to grow. The seed requires nourishment. It needs food and water to grow. There are nutrients contained in the soil that houses the seed; and water is supplied by either heaven, or by us. And just like that seed, faith must also be nourished and cultivated. Once our faith gets deeply rooted in the word of God, it begins to grow and produce fruit. Prayers are answered. Breakthroughs abound. Miracles happen. Healing and deliverance occurs because our faith is strong and firmly established on a solid foundation — the word of God.

Jesus, being pursued by a crowd, had compassion on them and took time to minister to them, and healed all that had need of healing. When it began to get late, Jesus' disciples told Him to send the crowd away (about 5,000 men, not including women and children) so they could go into the towns and buy food for themselves. Jesus, being full of faith, said to His disciples, "you give them something to eat." But the disciples said, "we don't have enough to feed this great crowd; we only have two small fish and five loaves of bread." Jesus, commanding the disciples to have the crowd sit down, took the two fish and five loaves of bread, looked up to heaven, and blessed and gave thanks for it, then gave it to His disciples and told them to distribute the food to the people. Jesus miraculously multiplied those two small fish and five loaves of bread to feed all 5,000 people, with enough fragments left over to fill twelve baskets *(Luke 9:10-17)*.

The disciples were thinking logically. In their minds, it was not possible to feed a crowd of 5,000 with two fish and five loaves of bread. But Jesus, being full of the Holy Ghost, was not looking at the situation logically. He was looking through the eyes of faith. When we look through the eyes of faith, we can see the impossible as possible. Jesus, by faith, was able to work a miracle with the fish and the loaves.

A miracle, again, is some event or phenomenon that goes against the laws of nature. Under normal circumstances it is not possible. But with God, *all* things are possible! If we have faith in God, and believe that the impossible is possible, "all things are possible to him that believes" *(Mark 9:23)*.

Are you facing an impossible-looking situation? Begin to see it through the eyes of faith. Begin to see it as possible with God, and watch the "impossible" happen.

DOUBT

Doubt is probably one of the biggest barriers to faith. What is doubt? The *Noah Webster 1828 Dictionary* defines doubt as follows: To waver or fluctuate in opinion, to hesitate; to fear or to be apprehensive; to question.

When you doubt, you are uncertain. You do not have full confidence, therefore you hesitate. You begin to waver between two minds, never fully committing to one or the other. The thing has not yet been settled in your spirit.

Doubting is like the wind, blowing and shifting, never fully coming to a complete rest. Everything in the path of the wind, which is not rooted down, gets blown away. Doubt, just like the wind, blows everything in your mind away, never allowing you to grab hold of it, preventing it from taking root. It is the seeds of doubt in your mind that begin to take root, and bloom, and eventually tower over all your hopes and dreams, making them cloudy and barely visible.

You should be planting seeds of faith in your mind, not seeds of doubt. Once these faith seeds are cultivated and nourished, and become rooted and grounded in the word of God, they begin to shoot up and eventually tower over all doubt so that everything else becomes dwarfed by faith. It is faith, then, that begins to be dominant and powerful in your life. Your goal should be to have faith dominate everything in your life.

Doubt can also paralyze you with fear, making it impossible for you to believe. You want to believe God's word is true, but you are afraid of how you might look if the thing you have told people you are believing for doesn't come to pass. You are afraid of what people might say, or concerned that they may begin to question your faith, and consequently, your walk with God. So, you think it's simply easier not to believe rather than to believe and be disappointed if you don't see results. The Bible reminds us that "God has not given us the spirit of fear; but of power, and of love, and of a sound mind" *(2 Timothy 1:7)*. You must rebuke the spirit of fear whenever it begins to rise up in your spirit because fear is of the devil, not of God. Fear is a great hindrance to faith. In order to walk in faith, you must not doubt.

Abraham did not doubt when God told him he

would have a son, and that He would bless Abraham, and make him the father of nations. Abraham was 100 years old at the time, and Sarah, his wife, was 90. But Abraham did not stagger at the deadness of Sarah's womb or the deadness of his own body. He simply believed. And God blessed him. Abraham had a son (Isaac), and became the father of nations, just as God had promised.

God wants us to simply believe—not wavering, not doubting. If He promised it, He is well able to bring it to pass. Believe with all your heart, and do not doubt.

PERSISTENT WORRYING

I used to always say, "I'm just a worrier by nature." I used to confess this out loud. This was my way of justifying my persistent worrying. I used to worry about everything. Most of the things I worried about I had no control over anyway, but I worried just the same. This is often the case with worriers; they worry about things they have no control over, which only intensifies the worrying.

Worry is closely related to doubt. You are uncertain, therefore you worry. You are fearful, therefore you doubt. It all creates a vicious cycle, which, unless you learn to control it, can quickly get out of hand.

God wants us to be free of worry and doubt. He wants us to learn to lay everything at His feet, and leave it there. When we worry, we are in essence saying that we don't trust God to take control of our lives. We don't trust Him to work things out for us. And we don't have faith in who He says He is—a burden bearer, a way maker, a problem solver, a healer, and a deliverer. Worry causes us to question God: His sovereignty, and His supernatural power. This is another barrier to faith. You can't have faith in God when you question who He is, or worry if He is able to move in your life.

Faith requires you to have complete confidence in God, and His power. Faith demands that you not worry if God is willing and/or able; just believe that He is. You will begin to see things happen for you when you stop worrying, and start believing. God is willing and able to do what He says He can do. All you have to do is simply believe.

אֱמוּנָה
FAITH

Chapter 24

THE ROAD TO FAITH

The road to faith is never easy. You will experience pitfalls and setbacks along this road. There will be opposition along the way. At times, you may feel as though you can't go on—when you feel like quitting, or throwing in the towel. But please do not throw in the towel yet; there is hope.

Although this journey may not be easy, it is necessary.

The Bible tells us that without faith it is impossible to please God *(Hebrews 11:6)*. We must have faith, for faith pleases God. We are all given a measure of faith; it is up to us to cultivate that faith so that it grows and produces fruit. This fruit in turn encourages us to continue in faith, and helps others to believe, building up their faith and drawing them to God. The ultimate outcome of our faith is for God to get the glory. When others see us walking by faith, and see the results and rewards of our faith, it should cause them to believe and turn to God. The end result should always lead to the Lord being glorified.

JESUS LEADS THE WAY TO FAITH

Jesus is the author and finisher of our faith. He is the ultimate perfecter of faith. He led the way, giving us the perfect example to follow when it comes to faith. Jesus often let it be known that He came to earth on a mission. His mission was to do the will of His Father.

"Jesus saith unto them, My meat is to do

> the will of him that sent me,
> and to finish his work."
>
> (John 4:34)

It is impossible to travel down this road of faith and not encounter Jesus. Jesus had pure faith. He understood His mission. He also knew He was empowered by God to successfully complete this mission, understanding He only had a short time to complete it. Therefore, Jesus remained focused and dedicated, and sure of the God who had sent Him.

Jesus had His share of detractors. There were many people who questioned His right to say and do some of the things He said and did. Who is this guy? Where did He come from? How can a carpenter's son claim to be the Son of God?

Jesus went against protocol and that turned people off, especially the Pharisees, who were often His biggest critics. He often broke away from traditional Jewish customs. He sat with sinners and publicans, who were often hated by the Jews because they collected taxes for the Roman government, which were seen as a burden. Jesus ate with unwashed hands. He performed miracles on the Sabbath. This all made many uncomfortable and a little suspicious of Him. He did not meet their expectations of what a good Jew should be. But Jesus shattered the mold, and tore up the script, and set a new standard, which was open for all to follow—both Jews and Gentiles. Faith requires us to tear up the old script that has governed our decisions and actions our entire lives. We must go against established protocol, and be willing to step out from under the expectations of others in order to live a life of faith.

Jesus was also unconventional. He went up to the mountain for extended periods to pray. He hung out with people who were often viewed as outcasts, and social rejects. Some, wore camel's skin, and ate locusts and wild honey. Others washed His feet with their tears. Many were prostitutes, beggars, and people who were considered unclean by Jewish standards. This was not your typical cast of characters that a good Jew, in those days, would normally associate with. But Jesus was open to all. He knew His mission involved helping these people — reaching out to them, and ultimately drawing them to the Father. He had compassion on them, and saw them through the eyes of love. This compassion drew Jesus to these people instead of repelling Him away from them. He knew that in order to help them, He had to reach out to them; and that's exactly what He did. Jesus' love was like a magnet, drawing people to Him, and ultimately into a loving relationship with God.

Jesus' ministry also brought Him into contact with the elite (i.e., the rulers of the synagogues, and the upper echelon of Roman society). He, however, was not impressed with their positions and power. Jesus knew that in order to be the greatest in the kingdom of heaven, you had to humble yourself, leave the comforts of home, family, material possessions, and take up your cross and follow Him. It could cost you everything to follow Jesus. But you must be prepared to sacrifice all in order to walk down this road of faith — this road that Jesus walked.

The faith road is not a road to gain popularity. People will despise you, and speak ill of you. Jesus was often rejected. Some only wanted to associate with Him because of the miracles and whatever benefits they thought they might derive from Him. But they, unlike Him, were unwilling to give up anything, or to sacrifice for the kingdom of heaven's sake. Jesus was willing to pay the ultimate price, and thus He gave up His life to accomplish the Father's will.

If you are not ready to sacrifice everything for God, you are not ready to live a life of faith. Understand, this life is not for the faint of heart. You may lose some friends. And you may even experience rejection. But faith dictates that you often go it alone, going against the grain instead of going along with the crowd — like a salmon swimming upstream against the currents. This, however, is not always easy. But if you remain faithful, you will be rewarded in the end.

Be prepared to be called a freak, unusual, or abnormal. People could not understand Jesus. He did not appear normal to them — at least not according to their definition of normal anyway. They may have even thought He was a lunatic. What kind of person claims to be born of a virgin? Who confesses to being the Son of God? Wouldn't it be easier to say that you were the son of Joseph? This wouldn't have caused quite the stir that confessing to being the Son of God did. But Jesus didn't come to please men. Nor was He interested in denying who He was. As Jesus often said, we must be about our Father's business. Each of us were created for a purpose. We are called and anointed to finish His work on the earth, and to do even greater works.

Yes, Jesus set the standard for faith. He perfected it. He showed us how to operate in it. He acted on His faith. He performed many miracles, healed everyone who had the faith to be healed, and left a multitude of delivered folk, who otherwise would have remained in bondage. Now it is up to you and I to walk out our faith. We must finish Jesus' work. There are still people today who are bound by the enemy that need to be set free. "And greater works than these shall he do" *(John 14:12).*

FAITH COMES BY HEARING

Faith comes by hearing, and hearing by the word of God *(Romans 10:17)*. In order to believe, or to know something, you must first hear about it. It is virtually impossible to form an opinion about something you've never heard of. You must first be made aware of it, then you expand your knowledge on the subject by researching to find out more about it. You may even listen to other people's opinion on the subject, but ultimately, you form your own opinion.

Faith is a topic you often hear discussed in Christian circles. Everyone has an opinion about faith, and knows that faith is important for the believer. We are told that we must have faith. But I've never really heard anyone tell us *how* to have faith. They just simply say, you must have faith, or, just believe.

It was not until I started earnestly reading the Bible, and praying to God, that I started to get a revelation of faith—of what it is, and how it works. While reading God's word, my spiritual eyes began to open as the Holy

Ghost revealed faith to me. There are many examples in the Bible of people who had great faith. But just reading the stories alone—although they do encourage you to want to walk in faith!—does not explain to you *how* to have faith. It takes the Holy Ghost to reveal faith to you, making it a concept you can grasp. As faith grows in you, it becomes real to you; this makes it tangible. Once faith becomes real to you, you can then start walking by faith.

Abraham walked by faith; he lived it out in a visible way. The Bible says that Abraham simply believed God. When God said to Abraham, "I'm going to bless you and make you the father of nations," Abraham did not scratch his head and say, "But how are you going to do that seeing I am old, and my wife, Sarah, is past child-bearing age?" No, but when God spoke, he simply believed (once he had gotten over the initial shock of it all). He didn't worry about his body or Sarah's dead womb; this isn't an issue—not when God speaks. Abraham believed God,

> **ABRAHAM WALKED BY FAITH.**

and in His ability to do what He promised He would do—bless him!—not in his own ability to produce a child.

Once you begin to know God—to become acquainted with Him—your spiritual eyes begin to open, and you begin to see God for who He is. And once you know Him, over time, you begin to trust Him. Most of us have trust issues. It is hard for us to trust people because we have been hurt, disappointed, and let down many times by people. But we cannot equate God with people. There is just no comparison. Don't put God in the same box with the people who have let you down. God is a God in whom we can trust—period! We can trust Him with our hearts, our lives, and with everything we have.

God will not lie to us: "God is not a man, that he should lie; neither the son of man, that he should repent: hath he said, and shall he not do it?" *(Numbers 23:19)*. Has He said it? Doesn't God's word offer certain promises to those who obey Him, and walk upright before Him? If He said it, you can trust that He will bring it to pass. When God speaks, simply believe. Don't look at the situation; look at God. This is what Abraham did. He did not look at the obvious limitations within himself or Sarah. He looked at God and His power, and His ability to perform everything He said He would do; and because of this, Abraham was blessed, and became the father of nations, as God had promised.

Faith looks at God, not the situation. Faith knows that God is All-Powerful, All-Seeing, and All-Knowing. When you look at God through the eyes of faith, you begin to see the impossible as possible. You begin to see who He is—a miracle-working God. And you begin to expect a miracle. When you expect a miracle, you start preparing for it, talking about it, and seeing it manifested in your life.

So today, I encourage you to get into the word of God like never before. Study God's word daily. Meditate on it. Begin to eat, sleep, and breathe the word of God. Because, it is only when you know God, and His word, that your faith will grow, and start to produce fruit. Ask God to reveal Himself to you through His word, and watch Him do it!

FAITH COMES BY DOING - ACTIVATE YOUR FAITH!

There was a woman in Galilee, in the country of the Gadarenes, who had an issue of blood (a hemorrhage) for twelve years. Imagine bleeding internally and uncontrollably for twelve long years, and feeling hopeless. She had gone to several doctors spending all her living, hoping they could help her stop the flow of bleeding. But none of the doctors could heal her.

She was desperate for a cure. She knew that if she didn't get help soon, she could possibly die. One day, she happened upon a crowd of people who were surrounding Jesus, to the point where they were almost suffocating Him. They were all trying to get close to Him. They had apparently heard of the many miracles Jesus had performed, and of the numerous people He had healed. They were all in desperate need of something, and recognized that He might very well be their only hope.

This woman with the issue of blood was also in

desperate need of a touch from Jesus. So she pressed her way through the crowd—through the throng of people surrounding Jesus—and reached out and touched the hem of His garment. And immediately, her hemorrhage dried up; she was instantly healed.

Jesus, recognizing that healing power had gone forth from Him, stopped and asked the crowd, "Who touched me?" When all denied touching Him, Peter said, "Master, the people are crowding and pressing in on You." But Jesus knew that someone had touched Him; He knew that this touch was a different touch from the press of the crowd. This touch extracted power from Him. When the woman saw that she could no longer hide, she came and fell down before Jesus, trembling, and admitted that she had indeed touched Him. She explained her situation, and told Him that the moment she touched Him she was healed. Jesus, having compassion on her, said to her, "Daughter, your faith has made you well; go in peace" *(Luke 8:42-48)*.

This woman activated her faith. She had a need, and recognized that Jesus may be her only hope for healing.

She did not let the crowd stop her from getting to Jesus; she pressed her way past the crowd. Nor did she wait for Jesus to notice her; she reached out to Him, which activated His healing power. The moment she did - the moment she reached out to Him in faith - she was healed.

This is an example of faith in action. She believed, therefore she moved forward with action to touch Him, believing that when she did, her blood condition would be healed. The healing power of Jesus Christ immediately connected with her faith, and she was healed in that very moment.

We must activate our faith, just as this woman did, in order to connect with the power source: Jesus Christ. How can we say we have faith when we have never put it into action? Faith is a verb; it's an action word. Faith does not cause you to sit idly on the sidelines. Faith causes you to roll up your sleeves, get in there and play. That would be like me saying that I am a basketball player, but every time you come to the games all you ever see me do is sit on the sidelines, and watch others play. But I never play. You might eventually begin to question whether I really am a basketball player. How can you say you play basketball, when you never play?

Likewise, how can we say we have faith when we never put it into action? We must put action to our faith for it to make the connection with God's power. Activate your faith, and watch God begin to move in your life. God's power meets you at the point of your faith. It's that contact that ignites God's power—like a stick of dynamite coming into contact with a match. The dynamite houses all this power, but it's only when you strike the match that the power in the dynamite is released. Release God's power; strike the match of faith, and watch what happens!

Similarly, faith is like a key that when inserted into the ignition and turned, releases all the power housed in the engine. But if you never insert the key, the power sits there idle. It's there, but if you never activate the switch, the power will never be released. When we release God's power through faith, we receive what we're believing God for. When we release His power, great things begin to happen for us. Release God's power today.

אֱמוּנָה
FAITH

Chapter 25

JESUS' FAITH IN ACTION

The Bible speaks of many great *patriots of faith:* Abraham, Moses, Noah—the list goes on and on. But I would like to talk about Jesus—who, in my opinion, is the greatest example of faith we have. It is ultimately His example that we should follow.

Jesus, being born of God when He overshadowed Mary with His Spirit, took on sinful flesh, and came to earth as a man. When He walked the earth, He was in every way a man as we are (yet without sin!), and often referred to Himself as the Son of Man, which was His way of acknowledging His humanity, and it also showed His humility. Jesus was also tempted, as we are. He grew weary after traveling a great distance, on His way to Galilee, when He sat down at a well and had a prophetic encounter with a Samaritan woman. He became angry when He went into the Temple and saw what they were doing in His Father's house, and threw them all out. Jesus was even baptized and filled with the Holy Ghost, because He knew it was required of Him to fulfill all righteousness. The things Jesus did—when He took on a human body—were all done under the power of the Holy Ghost. Therefore, those of us who have received this same power—after receiving the gift of the Holy Ghost—are able to do the same things Jesus did, by faith; and greater works shall we do.

WALKING ON WATER

After feeding a group of 5,000, Jesus instructed His

disciples to get into a boat, and go on ahead of Him while He sent the multitude away. When the people had dispersed, Jesus went alone into the mountain to pray. When evening had come, and the disciples were already a great distance from land, Jesus came to them, walking on the water. When they saw Him, they were afraid, assuming it was a ghost. He calmed them and told them not to be afraid, "It is I." Peter, quickly recovering from his fear, wanted to do what Jesus did and asked Jesus to command him to come to Him on the water. Jesus commanded, and Peter began to walk on the water toward Jesus. But, when Peter saw the strong wind he was afraid and began to sink. Jesus then stretched out His hand to save Peter, and both Peter and Jesus got into the ship. Jesus began to chide him for doubting. Peter was able, by faith, to walk on the water — as Jesus had done — but quickly began to sink when he started to doubt.

Fear, which is the opposite of faith, will handicap your faith, causing it to become ineffective. Jesus, being full of faith, was able to walk on water. The thought probably never even occurred to Him that He *couldn't* walk on water. He simply believed that He could. And Jesus, being full of the Holy Ghost, put His faith into action when He struck out toward the lake, and started walking on the water. He conquered fear and doubt in that moment, and performed a miracle for all to see. Peter, seeing this miracle, briefly overcame his fear and was also able to walk on the water. But when Peter stopped looking at it through the eyes of faith, he began to sink. While he was in faith, the miracle was possible; but the moment he lost faith, it became impossible. Miracles will only become a reality for us when we start looking at our situation through the eyes of faith.

CALMING THE STORM

On a certain day, Jesus and His disciples got into a boat to go over to the other side of the lake. (Jesus always had ministry on His mind!) As they were going forward, Jesus fell asleep. And suddenly, there was a strong gust of wind that descended on the lake, and the boat began to fill with water, and they were in danger. When the disciples saw this they were afraid and went to wake Jesus saying, "Master, Master, we are perishing!" Jesus got up and rebuked the wind and the surging waves, and they stopped, and it became calm. Jesus said to them, "Where is your faith?" They, being fearful and amazed, began to ask one another, "who is this, that He commands even the winds and the water, and they obey Him?"

Jesus, being full of faith, and the Holy Ghost, spoke with authority to the winds and the water, and they obeyed Him. They, responding to His faith, were immediately calm. This intrigued those around Him and they began to question who He was that He could perform such amazing feats *(Luke 8:22-25)*.

Jesus' faith was in action. He knew the power of God, and knew that nothing was by any means impossible to Him through faith. Jesus knew He had authority over the elements—the works of His own hands—for all things were created by Him, and for Him. He was also showing His disciples that nothing was impossible to the one who believes. If they simply believed in the power of God, they too could do the impossible—the impossible becomes possible!

RAISING THE DEAD

Jesus and His disciples, being accompanied by a great crowd, were on their way to Nain (a village of Galilee) when they came upon a funeral procession. A widow had lost her only son, and they were carrying him to his burial. When Jesus came upon this grieving mother, He had compassion on her, and said to her, "do not weep." He then went up to the coffin, causing those carrying him to stop, and touched the coffin. Speaking to the dead man He said, "Young man, I say to you, arise." And in response to Jesus' command, the young man sat up and began to speak.

Now, the Bible doesn't say what the young man said, but he could have said to Jesus, "I knew you'd come." Or, to his mother, "mom, don't cry: I'm here." Whatever he said, we know that this grieving mother was happy to have her son restored to her. This day, there was one less grieving mother in the city of Nain. And this day, Jesus proved to the world that by faith even the dead can be raised back to life. Death has to respond to faith and give up its victim. By faith, *nothing* is impossible to the one who believes.

On another occasion, Jesus raised another man, named Lazarus, from the dead. Lazarus and his two sisters, Mary and Martha, were dear friends of Jesus. Jesus loved them. Lazarus had fallen sick, and his two sisters sent a message to Jesus telling Him that the one He loved was sick. They wanted Jesus to come quickly and heal him. When Jesus received the message, He still remained where He was for another two days. During this time, Lazarus died. After two days, Jesus told His disciples they needed to go to Bethany because, "our friend Lazarus is asleep, but I am going there to wake him." Jesus spoke of Lazarus' death. But His disciples, not understanding what He meant, assumed He meant Lazarus was taking a rest, assuming that his rest would soon make him recover from his illness. But then Jesus, seeing they didn't understand, plainly said to them, "Lazarus is dead."

Before Jesus reached the city, someone told Martha that Jesus was on His way, and she ran to meet Him. Heavy with grief, she said to Him, "Master, if you had been here, my brother wouldn't have died. And even now I know that whatever you ask from God, He will grant it to you." Jesus told her that her brother would arise again. But she, not understanding what He meant, assumed He was referring to the resurrection at the last day, when Jesus will return for His church. But Jesus was referring to Lazarus' immediate resurrection from the dead; to which He responded, "I am the resurrection and the life. Whoever believes in me, although he may die, yet he shall live. And whoever continues to live and believes in me shall never die at all. Do you believe this?" Martha's response was, "yes, Lord, I have believed that you are the Christ, the Son of God, who was to come into the world." Then she ran to tell her sister Mary that the Master had come and was calling for her.

When Mary raced out to meet Jesus, in the same place where Martha had left Him, she fell down at His feet, weeping, and said to Him, "Lord, if you had been here, my brother would not have died." When Jesus saw her sobbing, and the Jews who came with her, He was deeply moved in spirit and troubled. When they took Him to Lazarus' grave, Jesus wept. He truly loved him.

But Jesus quickly recovered and commanded them to remove the stone from his grave. (By this time Lazarus had been dead four days, and they feared that by now there was a foul odor.) So they removed the stone, and Jesus looked up to heaven and said, "Father, I thank you that you have heard me. Yes, I know you always hear and listen to me, but I have said this on account of and for the benefit of the people standing around, so that they may believe that you did send me." When He had said this, He shouted with a loud voice, "Lazarus, come out!" And he, who was once dead, came walking out of the grave bound with grave clothes. Jesus commanded them to loose him. Upon seeing what Jesus had done in raising Lazarus from the dead, many of the Jews who had come with Mary believed in Him.

Jesus is the resurrection and the life. He has power over the living, and the dead. The dead must respond to His voice. There is power in no other name, than the name of Jesus Christ. This power is not something that is exclusive to Jesus only. He has transferred this same power to His church to use His name to speak life over the dead. And at the name of Jesus, the dead must respond. Life and death are in the power of the tongue. If we have the faith to believe, the miracles that Jesus did shall we do also. Nothing is impossible to us through faith. Faith even raises the dead back to life.

By faith, Jesus healed many people of various ailments and diseases. He cast out, and delivered many from demonic oppression and possession. He spoke prophetically into the lives of many, causing them to believe. Jesus was a walking, talking example of faith. He led the way that we should follow. He told His disciples, "Verily, verily, I say unto you, He that believeth on me, the works that I do shall he do also; and greater works than these shall he do; because I go unto my Father" *(John*

14:12).

We should follow Jesus' example of faith. We should pattern ourselves after His life and ministry, as He was operating in full faith, under the power of the Holy Ghost. And as He told His disciples (and us today), the works that He did shall we do also. Anything is possible to us by faith. Do you believe it? Then act on it. Activate your faith!

אֱמוּנָה
FAITH

Chapter 26

GREAT FAITH!

CENTURION SOLDIER

Capernaum is a city on the northwest shore of the Sea of Galilee. Jesus dwelt at Capernaum at the beginning of His ministry, and although He did much teaching and performed many miracles there, few people from Capernaum followed Jesus. So Jesus grieved over Capernaum for its lack of faith *(Matthew 11:20-24)*.

There was a centurion in Capernaum who had a servant who was highly regarded by him, who was sick and about to die. When he heard of Jesus, he sent some Jewish elders to Him to beg Him to come and heal his servant. When the elders came to Jesus, they earnestly implored Him saying that he was worthy that Jesus should do this for him.

A centurion was the highest rank one could reach in the Roman army. He often had one hundred soldiers under him. So he was a man of authority, and highly respected. This centurion had also built a Synagogue for them with his own money.

As Jesus was going with the Jewish elders, and when He was not far from the house, the centurion sent friends to meet Jesus, and to say to Him,

> "Lord, do not trouble Yourself further,
> for I am not worthy for You to come
> under my roof;

> for this reason I did not even
> consider myself worthy to come to You,
> but just say the word,
> and my servant will be healed.
> For I also am a man placed
> under authority,
> with soldiers under me; and I say
> to this one, 'Go!' and he goes,
> and to another, 'Come!' and he comes,
> and to my slave, 'Do this!'
> and he does it."
> (Luke 7:6-8)

Jesus marveled at the centurion, and turned to the crowd that was following Him and said, "I say to you, not even in Israel have I found such great faith." When the Jewish elders had returned to the house, they found the servant well and in good health.

Jesus was amazed by the centurion's faith, for he believed that all Jesus had to do was speak a word of healing over his servant, and he would be healed.

He did not need Jesus to come and lay His hands on his servant—he didn't believe it required any kind of physical contact. He believed that Jesus had the power to *speak,* and his servant would be healed. And that's exactly what happened, Jesus spoke, and he was healed in that very moment. This faith caused Jesus to marvel and to tell the crowd that this is what great faith looks like.

Great faith believes that Jesus has the power to do what you are believing Him to do. It removes any kind of limitations or barriers that we sometimes place on Jesus. It doesn't look at the situation as impossible; nothing is impossible when we walk by faith, and not by sight. Great faith pleases God and gets a response from Him. This kind of faith, although unusual, is not impossible. It is possible for us to have this kind of faith today. We can illicit a response from God by placing great faith in Him. Just begin to take the blinders off, and remove anything that might hinder you from walking in faith. Can you see it through the eyes of faith? Then you can have it. Can you believe without wavering or doubting?

Then all things are possible to you if you trust God, and never doubt.

Chapter 27

IF THE WORLD DOESN'T BELIEVE

If the world doesn't believe, it's our fault. If the world doesn't believe in the existence and the power of God, it's the church's fault. We've failed them. When the church is walking in the full power and authority of the living God, then the signs will follow; the signs will testify to the existence of a God who is working through us, behind-the-scenes, causing these great miracles, signs, and wonders to occur. When the church is operating according to the Scriptures, the world can't deny the existence of God because they see the signs, which are hard to deny.

When Peter and John healed the lame man by the temple gates, the chief priests and elders could not deny that a miracle had taken place, because they saw the evidence; but because they were jealous, they threatened them, commanding them not to preach or to teach in the name of Jesus. It's not that they didn't believe, it's that their hearts were hardened and they felt that their positions, and all the benefits they received from them, were in jeopardy. The world cannot deny the power of God when He is operating through His people. The church has failed God in this sense.

When we become too full of ourselves and our own importance, we neglect God and His work that He wants to perform on earth through us. When our focus is on the pursuit of worldly gain, and the accumulation of material possessions, we neglect God and our spiritual duties. We can't love the world and love God at the same time. Those who love the world, do not love God. And when we neglect our spiritual duties, the gospel is not being preached throughout the earth, and the enemy is allowed the opportunity to slip into that void and darken the hearts of men, using them as puppets for his own evil purpose.

Satan has darkened the hearts of men, and fooled them into believing they don't need God; that they can establish their own laws and govern themselves instead of obeying God's laws. In order to see what a heart absent from God looks like, all we have to do is look at the world around us. When there is no God-consciousness, evil prevails. When man tries to govern himself, of course he will only set up rules that are pleasing to him, rules that don't require much of him, and rules that allow him the freedom to do the things he wants to do. Our rules place our own best interest at the center. When there is no regard for God and His rules, the world suffers, because there is no accountability, no one to answer to, no one to take us by the hand and say, "you shouldn't have done that," or, "don't do that again, because that behavior is not acceptable."

God sees what we cannot see. He knows the things that are going on behind-the-scenes, in the spirit realm. He wants to protect us from these unseen forces, whose goal is to destroy man and to keep him from fulfilling his destiny—the destiny he was created to fulfill.

Daniel prayed, seeking an answer from God about the vision he had received regarding Israel. Daniel prayed and fasted petitioning God for an answer, and for grace and mercy on his and Israel's behalf. And God sent an answer to Daniel through his angel, Gabriel. But the answer was delayed because Gabriel was held up by the prince of the kingdom of Persia, who intercepted him while he was on his way to deliver God's response to Daniel. This warring prince withstood Gabriel for twenty-one days until Michael, one of the chief angels, came to help him; then Gabriel was freed to come to Daniel to deliver his message. God showed Daniel what would befall Israel because of their disobedience, and refusal to obey His laws *(Daniel 10)*.

There are things happening in the spirit realm that

we cannot see with our natural eyes. There are battles being fought between the forces of darkness and God's holy angels. Sometimes we may pray to God seeking an answer from Him about something that's troubling us, but His answer may be delayed because of a spiritual battle taking place behind-the-scenes. It's not that God doesn't hear our prayers — He hears us when we pray — sometimes His answer may be delayed, for various reasons.

Of course the forces of darkness want to stop your blessings from getting to you, knowing that some people will grow weary in waiting on God. Some will lose faith. And some will simply throw their hands up and walk away. But if we can learn to wait on God, no matter how long it takes, and keep trusting Him, no matter how things look, He will send us an answer in due time. Faith waits on God, being fully convinced that He is a God of His word.

The church must believe wholeheartedly in God, His holy word, and His omnipotent power. Partial belief is unbelief. We can't pick and choose the things we want to believe, and reject the things we don't understand, or the things we don't agree with. How can we expect the world to believe, if the church doesn't fully believe, submit, and obey? Our lackadaisical days are over. Either we are all-in, or we are all-out. But we cannot continue to straddle the fence with God. Our belief in God should cause us to lay down everything, and pick up our cross (the same burdens, tests, and trials Jesus endured), and follow Him.

Our example and devotion to God should lead others to the only God who can save them, forgive their sins, and heal them. We should lead the way when it comes to faith, obedience, and devotion to God. If the world doesn't know God, it's our fault. We should be boldly proclaiming the Gospel of Jesus Christ everywhere we go; and our lives should be a reflection of God's holy will for all of mankind.

Chapter 28

WHAT WOULD HAPPEN IF?

What would happen if the church was on fire for God, full of faith, and full of anointed power from God? Full of Holy Ghost power! Can you imagine with me? Imagine if the church took its call and commission very seriously. Imagine if the church boldly proclaimed the good news of the gospel throughout the world, not wavering, not doubting, not adding anything to it or taking anything away from it. Imagine the impact the preaching of the gospel would have on the world: lives would be forever changed. Men and women would be convicted of sin, and turn to God with a repentant heart. The unbeliever would become aware of God's existence through the preaching of the gospel, and the signs that follow the gospel.

Now imagine if the church was *full of the Holy Ghost*. Imagine if when God fills a believer up to overflowing with His Spirit, there is no room for pride, because, when we come in contact with the true and living God, we become aware of our insignificance before Him, and are immediately humbled and stripped of all self-righteousness. When we become filled up with God, there is no room for pride in our hearts because pride cannot inhabit the same space where the Holy Ghost dwells. Nor is there room for hatred in a heart that is filled with God. When we are full of the Holy Ghost, the love of God floods our hearts and we become changed in His presence. Our disposition changes, making us more like God. Love now becomes our signature trait, which is reflected in our good deeds, acts of service, and our love shown toward our fellow man.

When the church is full of faith in God, doubt cannot come in and control our lives, causing us to believe a lie over God. When we are walking in faith, the devil cannot put a wedge between us and God. When we are walking in the fullness of faith, we believe that anything is possible to the one who believes, and that nothing is impossible for our God. When faith rules our lives, we are no longer the servants of doubt. Doubt no longer enters the picture. And where there is unwavering faith in the power of God, miracles happen, which cause even more faith in God.

Imagine a world where everyone served God, and no one rejected Him. A world where everyone was obedient to God's laws, which are designed to keep peace and harmony with our fellow man, and with God. A world where everyone believed God's laws were more superior to man's laws. Under this system, there would be no murders, thefts, hatred, rape, child abuse, terrorism, gang violence, adultery, or spousal abuse. We would love and respect our fellow man and treat others the way we want to be treated. Our days would be filled looking out for our neighbors, serving others, lending a helping hand to those in need: the poor, the widow, and the orphan.

What would happen if Acts 13:44 became a reality in our city? "And the next sabbath day came almost the whole city together to hear the word of God." If an entire city could drop what they were doing and make their way to the house of the Lord, God's kingdom would be greatly multiplied, as souls were added to the church daily. There would be no room for the devil because Satan has no place in God's kingdom. Satan has no power to deceive and blind the hearts of men when the word of God is flowing in their hearts and minds. Satan's kingdom is destroyed when God's kingdom is elevated. If the entire city made their way to the house of God, what a glorious day that would be!

This may all sound idealistic on my part, but this is the world God originally created. This is the world He envisioned when He spoke the world into existence, causing the dry land to appear, the sun, the moon, and the stars to take their place in the sky, and when He formed man out of the dust of the ground and breathed into his nostrils the breath of life. This was God's plan for the earth when He created the heavens and the sea, giving space for His newly-created animals to fly and to swim, in their new habitat.

God envisioned a world where there would be love and peace and sweet communion between man and God. His new world would grow and prosper and never become dead and barren. There would be plenty of food for man and his furry friends to eat, with neither ever experiencing drought or lack. Everything would run smoothly, and everyone would be happy because everything God created was good.

But, then sin entered the picture and destroyed all the good that God had created. Everything you see going on in the world today, all the bad and the evil, is a result of man's disobedience and sin against God. Satan has taken what God has created and turned it into something wicked and twisted. But, the good news is that God will one day, soon, have an earth again that operates according to His original plan. For, He will soon destroy sin, removing its destructive force from the earth. He will also destroy this old sin-stained earth, and create a new earth, where Jesus will reign forever with His holy laws once again governing the earth.

> Revelation 21:
>
> 1 And I saw a new heaven and a new earth: for the first heaven and the first earth were passed away; and there was no more sea.
>
> 2 And I John saw the holy city, new Jerusalem, coming down from God out of heaven, prepared as a bride adorned for her husband.
>
> 3 And I heard a great voice out of heaven saying, Behold, the tabernacle of God is with men, and he will dwell with them, and they shall be his people, and God himself shall be with them, and be their God.
>
> 4 And God shall wipe away all tears from their eyes; and there shall be no

> more death, neither sorrow, nor crying, neither shall there be any more pain: for the former things are passed away.
>
> 5 And he that sat upon the throne said, Behold, I make all things new. And he said unto me, Write: for these words are true and faithful.

Amen (so be it). Comfort one another with these words.

אֱמוּנָה
FAITH

Chapter 29

MY WAKE-UP CALL

I spent the better part of my life working jobs that had no real value to me. They were mostly dead-end jobs, with little hope of ever leading to anything significant. I just went from one job to the next, never being able to shake that empty feeling I had inside. None of them brought me any real satisfaction. But through it all, I always knew deep-down inside that there had to be more. I was very much unfulfilled, and could not shake the feeling that God did not create me for this. He had a greater purpose for my life. But what that purpose was, at the time, I did not know.

I acknowledge the fact that throughout most of my "career" I was fighting to not allow myself to be forced into a mold along with everyone else. There is a tendency in companies (perhaps unconsciously) to have their employees all fit into a cookie-cutter mold. Every organization has a company culture—whether you realize it or not—and if you're not careful, you can find yourself conforming to that culture, at your own expense. In my opinion, this conforming limits individuality, snuffs out creativity, and most importantly, hinders a person's ability to hear God—who has created us to live a life of purpose, totally devoted and committed to Him.

The Bible says, "And be not conformed to this world: but be ye transformed by the renewing of your mind, that ye may prove what is that good, and acceptable, and perfect, will of God" *(Romans 12:2)*. Jesus Christ died so that we no longer have to conform to the world's standards. When we are born-again, we are set free from the chains that held us captive. We have been freed to live a life that is in-line with God's word, and according to His will for us. Why should we continue to live in bondage to the world when we no longer have to? Why not choose to live the life we were destined to live?

Well, I wanted to live the life I was destined to live, but I knew I wouldn't find it in any job, career, or otherwise. Nor did I want to conform to company culture, which, in my opinion, meant losing my unique identity in Christ, and taking on an identity given me by society. I knew God had created me for greater.

I saw an environment, in the corporate world, where people daily sacrificed themselves on the altar of corporate power. People were pushing and shoving, and clawing their way to the top in the hope of getting the most coveted prizes. I saw people lose the essence of who they were, trying to be like everyone else, or trying to live up to someone else's expectations. There was no spark in their eyes; family relationships often suffered; friends were lost; relationships with God soon became strained—and for what? A corner office with a view? The title of *Senior Vice President*? The respect and admiration of your peers? Really?!! Well, no thank you!

I needed to sustain myself. I fought very hard to maintain my true identity. It was a matter of life or death for me because I was afraid of losing *me*. Unfortunately, this mind-set does not gain you acceptance into this world. People may view you as a renegade, or a recluse, because you don't hob-knob with the masses, and because you don't attend the corporate parties where all the kissing up goes on. As a result, you may then be ostracized, and often passed over for promotions. But this was never important to me anyway. Now, please don't misunderstand: I went to work everyday and did my job well—but that's just what it was for me, a job, not a career, not my life. I did not define myself by what I could accomplish in the corporate world. A happy and wholesome family life, my relationship with God, and maintaining the *me* God created me to be, were more important to me than losing myself or compromising who I was to gain acceptance into this culture.

But God started calling me out of this environment long before I actually heeded the call. I started very vividly hearing God speak to me. He would simply say, "Trust God," and "God is your source." He was preparing me for the purpose and plan He had for me. He was preparing me for my destiny. And I heard Him, but I didn't really *hear* Him. I did not understand at the time exactly what He was trying to say to me. But I knew the Lord was trying to get my attention. So, I held onto these words over the years, not knowing that these very words would be the words that carried me through.

DON'T BECOME ATTACHED TO MATERIAL THINGS

Recently, God taught me a very important lesson: not to become too attached to material possessions. For the past eleven years, I had been dutifully taking my car to the same place to be serviced. But I decided this one time that I was going to take it somewhere else, hoping to save a little money. I was looking at two different places: one where I had recently gotten some new tires, and the other where they had done some minor work on my car. Both places told me they serviced my make of car. I just needed to decide to which of the two places I was going to take it.

When the time came to have my car serviced (I usually have it serviced once a year), I prayed, asking God which place I should take it to. (I believe in praying about everything!) I was leaning toward the place where I had gotten the new tires, but, God told me to take it to the other place. *You want me to take it there God; are you sure?* Now, I heard God speak the name of this place twice in my spirit, so this is where I decided to take it. Who am I to go against God?

This place had already sent me a postcard saying they could service my car. But when I called to make the appointment, I made sure I told them what kind of car I have so that they would know ahead of time that I was coming in (or tell me over the phone that they couldn't service my car). But the appointment was made, and the date was set.

When I arrived the morning of my appointment, I told the person behind the counter what type of oil I wanted—full synthetic—and he confirmed the price with me. After they finished servicing my car, and before I was about to drive off, I noticed that they hadn't reset the *oil service indicator light*. This light lets me know when it's time for an oil change. So, I went back inside and asked if they could please reset this for me. The guy behind the counter printed the instructions for how to reset the light, from online, and gave it to the technician to see if he could reset it (uh, oh..red flag!). The technician went outside and tried resetting the light, but couldn't get it to reset. After trying for a few minutes, he told me I should take it to where I normally have it serviced and have them reset it for me. (Well I could have taken it to them in the first place!) I wasn't happy, but I left there sort of regretting having taken my car there.

I made a couple stops on my way home. But before I actually made it home, the "Check Engine Oil Level" and the "Engine Oil Pressure" lights came on, and I also noticed my car's engine was running a little loud.

When I got home, I immediately called the place where I'd just had my car serviced, and asked what type of oil they'd put in my car. They told me they had used a synthetic blend. (I specifically asked for full synthetic!) I told them what was happening to my car, and they told me to bring it back in and they would drain the oil and put the right oil in.

Well, after I hung up with them, I called the place where I normally have my car serviced. And when I told them what had happened, they told me not to drive my car but to have it towed in. I debated whether to accompany the tow truck driver to the service department, and wait there until they had determined what was wrong with my car. But eventually, I decided not to accompany them there. I'll admit that I was a little reluctant to let my car go with the tow truck driver, but I decided that I wasn't going to sit there all day and *babysit* my car. I had other things to do.

When it was all said and done, they were able to determine what the problem was, and fix it. The other place had broken a part when they changed the oil, and without this part no oil was getting to the engine. The technician told me that it's a good thing I had the car towed in, because I could have damaged the engine if I had continued to drive it. In the end, I was without my car for two days.

I later began to wonder why God would tell me to take my car to this place. He had to know this would happen. (Because, of course, God knows all things!) He, of course, knew that this place really wasn't equipped to service my make of car, even though they said they were. I was actually considering taking it to the other place instead of this one. But, this is when I sensed God telling me in my spirit that He didn't want me to become too attached to material things. I was so attached to my car that I didn't want to let it out of my sight for one second. But, I had to release it, and just trust that God was going to take care of the situation for me.

The car is fine, and of course I will never take it to this place again. But I took to heart the lesson God was showing me through this whole incident: we should never become too attached to things. They are, after all, just things. Of course, we should take care of the things God blesses us with, but, we should not let them rule us or control our lives. And we should never place anything above God. We can't take any of it with us when we die, nor should we want to. I'm thanking God for this lesson, and for showing me where my heart was. When we focus too much on things, acquiring them and maintaining them, they can often become a stumbling block for us.

When the rich ruler came to Jesus and asked Him what he could do to inherit eternal life, Jesus told him that he should obey all the commandments: *do not commit adultery, do not kill, do not steal, do not bear false witness, honor your father and mother.* The man said, "all these have I kept from my youth up." (I'm sure he's feeling pretty good about himself right about now.) But Jesus said, "but there is yet one thing that you lack, sell all that you have and distribute unto the poor, and you shall have treasure in heaven: and come, follow me." When the young man heard this he was very sorrowful, because he was very rich. When Jesus saw his reluctance,

He said, "How hardly shall they that have riches enter into the kingdom of God! For it is easier for a camel to go through a needle's eye than for a rich man to enter into the kingdom of God" (*Luke 18:18-30*).

Jesus knew that those who have riches are often very attached to their wealth. It is very hard for them to part with their things. These things are what they have come to identify with; their self-worth is often tied to their things. This is why when some people lose everything they have, they kill themselves. They've lost all of their earthly possessions, and in their minds they have nothing left to live for, because they were only living for these things. Their goal in life was to accumulate wealth, and to maintain this wealth. So, if someone comes along, as Jesus did with the rich ruler, and tells them to give it all away, they couldn't imagine themselves living in this world without their much loved material possessions.

So, I'll ask you this question: If God were to tell you to give everything in your bank account to the poor, could you do it? What if He told you to sell off all your excess (to downsize), and to distribute the proceeds to the needy, could you do it? How attached are you to your things? Are your things holding you back from serving God with your whole heart?

WHEN GOD SPEAKS

When God speaks, we should be in a position to respond to His voice. But, if we are laden down with the cares of this world, it's very difficult for us to be used by God. God wants all of us: our hearts, our minds, our time, and our obedience. We should not be willing to withhold anything from Him. Open your hand and your heart wide, and be willing to give freely to those in need around you. The poor, the destitute, the widow, and the orphan all hold a special place in God's heart. He uses us to be a blessing to these people. When He blesses us, it's not just for us to enjoy, but for us to be a blessing to someone in need. God loves a cheerful giver.

When I first moved to the city I live in a few years ago, I was actively searching for a church home. I had already visited several churches when, one Sunday, I

He said, "How hardly shall they that have riches enter into the kingdom of God! For it is easier for a camel to go through a needle's eye than for a rich man to enter into the kingdom of God" (*Luke 18:18-30*).

Jesus knew that those who have riches are often very attached to their wealth. It is very hard for them to part with their things. These things are what they have come to identify with; their self-worth is often tied to their things. This is why when some people lose everything they have, they kill themselves. They've lost all of their earthly possessions, and in their minds they have nothing left to live for, because they were only living for these things. Their goal in life was to accumulate wealth, and to maintain this wealth. So, if someone comes along, as Jesus did with the rich ruler, and tells them to give it all away, they couldn't imagine themselves living in this world without their much loved material possessions.

So, I'll ask you this question: If God were to tell you to give everything in your bank account to the poor, could you do it? What if He told you to sell off all your excess (to downsize), and to distribute the proceeds to the needy, could you do it? How attached are you to your things? Are your things holding you back from serving God with your whole heart?

WHEN GOD SPEAKS

When God speaks, we should be in a position to respond to His voice. But, if we are laden down with the cares of this world, it's very difficult for us to be used by God. God wants all of us: our hearts, our minds, our time, and our obedience. We should not be willing to withhold anything from Him. Open your hand and your heart wide, and be willing to give freely to those in need around you. The poor, the destitute, the widow, and the orphan all hold a special place in God's heart. He uses us to be a blessing to these people. When He blesses us, it's not just for us to enjoy, but for us to be a blessing to someone in need. God loves a cheerful giver.

When I first moved to the city I live in a few years ago, I was actively searching for a church home. I had already visited several churches when, one Sunday, I decided to visit a church that was across the street from where I was living at the time. I'm always hesitant to attend a new church because you just never know what you're going to find. But I subsequently began to visit this particular church several times, and began to take note of some of the things they were doing. They had a passion for missions, and I couldn't help but notice a spirit-of-excellence in the church. Prayer was also a focus for this church, which had a very well-organized prayer ministry in place. I gravitated toward the prayer ministry, and got more involved.

As I was praying one day, I said to God that this particular church seemed to be *good ground*. And as soon as I said that, I heard the Lord whisper in my spirit, *100 thousand*. Well, this caught me completely off guard, and I remember jumping a little, and it felt as if my heart skipped a beat. But I clearly heard the Lord speak. And I knew what the Lord was saying; He was telling me to give $100,000 to this church. It was a whisper, but it was unmistakably God's voice speaking to my spirit. When you develop a relationship with God you begin to know

His voice.

Over the next several days, I began to seek "further confirmation" from God about what He had clearly asked me to do. This is what we often do. Even though we know God has told us to do a certain thing, we want to be absolutely certain that this is *really* God, and that we didn't just imagine it. During this period, I think I really expected God to speak to me again (to repeat what He had already said). But God said no more about it—He had *already* spoken.

This is when the tug-of-war began in my spirit. I knew what God had asked me to do, but my flesh, my rationalizing mind was saying, don't do it. *If you give this money, what will you live on?* Now, I had this money in the bank at the time, but it didn't make sense to my natural senses to part with it, because, what if an emergency comes up? What if later on down the road you need this money? (What if?.. What if?.. What if?..) This is when the words God had spoken to me years earlier came back to me. This is when I remembered what God had spoken to me—probably in preparation for this moment—when He said, "God is your source." "Trust God." Yes, trust God indeed. We *say* we trust Him, but do we really? I had to decide right then and there if I was going to trust God, or if I was going to put more trust in the money I had in the bank. Well, I decided to trust God.

This church that God told me to give this $100,000 to had a ministry for the support of widows, and they were planning to build a home for widows. Being a widow myself, I have great compassion for those who have lost a spouse. And as I stated before, God also has a special place in His heart for widows. So, trusting God, and that He is a God of His word, I wrote a check for $100,000 to go toward the building of this home for widows.

When God speaks, we should pay attention. God is not trying to *take* from us. He's actually trying to bless us. God did not ask me to give this money because He wanted to drain my bank account. I truly believe God was testing me, to see if He could trust me.

Moses told Israel: *God has taken you through this wilderness to test you, to see what's in your heart; to see if*

He can trust you or not. God had promised Israel a land of their own, flowing with milk and honey, and full of all good things. It was a land of abundance; a land where there was no lack. It was also a land where He would dwell among them. He would be their God, their source, their strength, and their protector. But, God needed to know if He could trust them with His blessings. Would Israel remain faithful to Him, or would they turn away from serving Him after He had flooded them with an abundance of blessings? We all know what happened: Israel did *not* pass the test. They spent 40 years in the wilderness murmuring and complaining against God. They turned away from Him to serve other gods. They were disobedient, and refused to obey His commandments. They proved to God that they could not be trusted with His blessings.

We want God to bless us, but, can God *trust* us with His blessings? Would we be like Israel: ungrateful, disobedient, unfaithful? Or, would we be like the rich ruler: too attached to our material possessions to part with them because we place more value in the riches of this world, than we value the riches of heaven? *Can* God trust you with His blessings?

BE A WISE STEWARD

I want to always be a wise steward over the blessings God entrusts me with. We should always be faithful stewards over God's blessings. I know that I haven't *always* been a wise steward, and have at times been wasteful. I wasn't one to create a budget and stick with it. I haven't always sought the better deal when making both major and minor purchases. I've bought things just because I saw them and wanted them, and not because I needed them (haven't we all done this?!). These spur-of-the-moment purchases add up. And this money could have been spent on a worthy cause, not on something that's going to collect dust on a shelf or get pushed to the back of the closet, and forgotten.

I see this now, and I am now more thoughtful when making purchases. Now, I will search to see if I can find a better deal on an item before making a purchase.

The Internet makes this easy today. You no longer have to drive all over town, going from place-to-place in search of a good deal. Now, all you have to do is a little research online. Most stores have a weekly circular on their website featuring all of their sale-priced items. This is a good place to start.

This is another lesson God has been teaching me: to be a wise steward over His blessings, not being wasteful or careless with the resources (be it money, or time) He blesses me with. We should always see all of these things as valuable, and not to be wasted.

Jesus tells a parable, in Luke 19, about a certain nobleman who went to a distant country to receive a kingdom for himself, and then to return. Prior to leaving, he called together ten of his servants and gave to each a mina (equal to about one hundred days' wages), telling them to buy and sell with it while he's away.

When he returns, after having received his kingdom, he calls his ten servants and asks each of them to give an account of what they've done with the money. The first one comes forward and says, "Lord, your mina has made ten additional minas." To which the nobleman responds, "well done, excellent bond servant! Because you have been faithful and trustworthy in a very little thing, you shall have authority over ten cities." The second one also comes and says, "Lord, your mina has made five more minas." And he says to this servant, "and you will take charge of five cities." Then another servant comes and says, "Lord, here is your mina, which I have kept laid up in a handkerchief. For I was afraid of you because you are a stern man." The nobleman responds, "you wicked slave! Why did you not put my money in the bank so that on my return, I might have collected interest?" And he takes the one mina and gives it to the one who has ten. Jesus then says to the crowd, "I tell you that everyone who gets and has will more be given, but from the man who does not get and does not have, even what he has will be taken away."

This parable can be interpreted in several ways. One, from a spiritual perspective. The nobleman, being a reflection of Jesus, who has gone away to prepare His kingdom to receive the church unto Himself. When He returns to earth to collect His church, He will reward those who have been faithful with what He has left in their hands: the building of the church, and the preaching of the gospel.

One might also view this parable from a natural perspective. We have each been entrusted with financial resources, and it is up to us to be faithful over what has been placed in our hands. Do we waste our resources on frivolous things? Or, do we responsibly make purchases, and wise investments that generate a return on what we have? Do we generously give to the poor, or do we neglect our duties to help those in need?

No matter how much or how little we have, we all have a responsibility to be faithful over the little, or the much, that has been placed in our hands. God expects us to be wise stewards, not wasteful or slothful. He wants to know that He can trust us to be faithful with the blessings He has so graciously given to us.

Israel wasn't faithful, and they had to suffer the consequences. They could have immediately entered the promised land after God brought them out of Egypt, but because of their unruly behavior, and their disobedience to God, they were made to wander forty years in the wilderness, delaying their entry into the land God had prepared just for them.

Jesus has gone away to prepare a home for us in heaven, where we will live with Him for eternity. But, what are we doing here on earth while we await His return? Are we obeying God's commandments? Are we remaining faithful to Him, or are we serving other gods (money, material possessions, etc.)? God will reward all those who remain faithful to Him. When you stand before God, and He asks you to give an account of everything He has placed in your hand, do you think His response will be, *well done!*, or will it be, *you wicked servant!*?

TRUST IS A TWO-WAY STREET

Not only does God want to know if He can trust us, He also wants to know if we trust Him. Trust goes both ways.

Last year, I was looking for a bookshelf for my books. I had been storing all of my books in boxes, and wanted a bookshelf so that they would be more easily accessible. I wanted something that wasn't big and bulky, and something that would be easy to move when it came time to move. I would occasionally search the stores and online, but everything I saw was either too big, too heavy, or too expensive. I must have searched off-and-on for months, never finding anything that fit my needs.

One day, I suddenly felt an urge to go to this certain store. I like this store because they have a lot of unique items; but, they can also be on the expensive side. On this day, I made my way over to the household items, and while browsing the selection, I came across a foldable bookshelf. At first glance, I didn't recognize it to be a bookshelf because it was rather unique. But upon further inspection, I discovered that it was indeed a bookshelf. I liked that it wasn't very big, and that it was easily transportable, should I need to move it. Even better was the price; it happened to be on sale for $30!

All the other bookshelves I had seen cost anywhere from $100 to $500, and up. And none of them fit my need. But this one was perfect, and the price was right.

Because this bookshelf was so affordable, I searched the store to see if there was another one like it, but there was not. So, I immediately made my purchase and loaded it into my car. But before going home, I decided to drive across town to see if I could find this same bookshelf at the store across town. Luckily, they also had one, and it was also on sale for $30! So I purchased this one too, and loaded it into my car. Two bookshelves for $60! You can't beat that.

Once again, God had blessed me with a desire of my heart. Now, although I was actively searching for a bookshelf off-and-on, I had not specifically prayed to God about it. But, being God, He knew the desire was there. And He knew that the exact type of bookshelf I was looking for was sitting at this store, on sale. So He, being the loving God that He is who loves to give His children the desires of their hearts, placed it in my heart to go to this particular store, on this particular day. It was no coincidence; it was divinely orchestrated by the Lord. God cares about even the small things when it comes to His children. He's a wonderful, loving Father.

When I arrived back at home, as *soon* as I walked through the door, the Lord said to me, *do you trust me?* Once again, His voice caught me off guard, and I think I had a *Peter moment*. The Peter moment being: after Jesus had told Simon Peter and his crew to cast out their net into the water to receive a great catch of fish, they came to shore dragging their net, which contained a multitude of fish, to find a feast that Jesus had prepared for them.

After they had eaten, Jesus said to Peter, "do you love me more than these?" Peter said, "yes, Lord; you know that I love you." Then Jesus said to him, "feed my lambs." Jesus asked Peter a second time, "Simon, son of Jonas, do you love me?" Peter responded, "yes, Lord; you know that I love you." Jesus again said, "feed my sheep." When Jesus asked Peter a third time if he loved Him, Peter became grieved because Jesus asked him this a third time. Peter responded, "Lord, you know all things; you know that I love you." Jesus said to Peter a third time, "feed my sheep."

So, when I walked through my door and heard the Lord ask me, *do you trust me?*, I became a little grieved and began to wonder why the Lord was asking me if I trusted Him. My response was similar to Peter's: *Lord, you know that I trust you.*

But God wants to know that we trust Him, not just with lip-service, with our actions revealing anything other than trust. Do we trust God to be a God of His word? Do we trust Him to meet our needs? Do we trust Him in the impossible-looking situations? Do we trust Him with the small things? Do we trust Him enough to take our hands off the wheel?

It's easy to say we trust God: when our bills are paid; when we have a steady income coming in; when we have health insurance through our employer, and we can go to the doctor anytime we want; when we have money in the bank; when we can go to the government for assistance in times of need; and when we can tap into the various resources that are available for those who have fallen on hard times. But, is this really trust in

God, or more in the confidence we have in the resources that are available to us? What would happen if none of these resources were available to us?

There are people in third-world countries who don't have any of these resources in place to be a crutch for them to lean on. They don't have government assistance, or money in the bank, or health insurance when they get sick. They don't have money to send their kids to school. Most don't even have clean water to drink, or they have to walk for miles to find water. And because their resources are so limited, they usually have to put their full trust and confidence in God to meet their needs.

You never hear any of these people saying, "God is not real." They *know* He's real, because they pray to Him everyday. They rely on Him because they can't rely on anyone else. Only in a land where people have come to depend on themselves, and in their own abilities to meet all of their needs, do you find people denying the existence of God. Only in a land where people have become accustomed to excess, and waste, do you hear people saying, "I don't need God in my life."

Maybe we've become so spoiled that we don't know what trust in God is. Maybe we've gained so many things that we've forgotten the times when we *had* to trust in God. The times when our resources were few. The times when we had to work very hard scraping and saving, and still barely getting by. Or, the times when we didn't throw things away when we got tired of them, or because they became old and worn, but repaired them and refurbished them, making them look like new again.

Maybe we've forgotten how hard our parents had to work, or their parents before them, to purchase a car, a home, or to put their kids through college. We've come a long way from these times, and how easy it is for us to forget where we've come from. God was the center of our lives then. We put our trust in Him to meet our needs when we didn't see a way. Our relationship with Him, then, was pure and genuine. We never pushed Him aside; He was always at the center of our lives.

God wants His children to trust Him. He is a God

who can be trusted. He's proven Himself to us time and time again. Never forget the things that God has already done for you through the years; use these things to propel you into further trust and confidence in God.

GOD WOULDN'T PUT MORE ON US THAN WE CAN BEAR

I've often heard people say, "God wouldn't put more on you than you can bear." Usually when people say this they mean that God wouldn't allow you to suffer or to experience hardships more than you are able to bear. This is a phrase Christians often use to comfort other Christians who are experiencing difficulties in their lives. They want these people to believe that if God has allowed it, then He knows that you are able to bear it. It is a phrase that has often been spoken to me. And although it is not Scripture, I understand what these people were trying to say: That no matter how difficult the situation is, God will always give us strength to bear it.

But one day, I began to see this phrase from a slightly different perspective: *God wouldn't put more on you than you can bear.* Although we usually mean God wouldn't put more *difficulties* on you than you can bear, I began to see that God also wouldn't put more *blessings* on you than you can bear.

There was an older couple in our church, who had to have been in their seventies at the time. The husband's mother also attended the church, and the three of them would ride to church together. You could see the love this couple had for each other. The wife would often call her husband "Daddy," which I thought was very sweet. They had been married for about 50 years, which is an amazing testament to the power of love. But, the husband had recently been diagnosed with cancer—I believe it was prostate cancer. You could clearly see the wife's love and devotion for her husband as she so lovingly cared for him, tending to his every need. She was also caring for his elderly mother, assisting her with her daily needs.

I remember one Sunday after church seeing all three

of them getting into their car. It was an older model two-door car. The wife and her mother-in-law sat in the front seat, with the husband climbing into the backseat. Watching this older, sick gentleman climb into a two-door car was not a pretty sight. I thought to myself: *they need a four-door car.*

As I was walking away, I felt the Lord was telling me to give them my car. Now, this was the only car I had at the time, but it was a newer-model than the one they were driving — it was maybe five years old at the time — and it was a four-door.

Not too long after this, I finished my Bachelor's degree, and as a graduation present to myself I decided to buy myself a new car. Instead of trading my car in, I decided to keep it and give it to this older couple. They were pleasantly surprised. I told them that I believed God wanted me to give them this car. The wife couldn't stop thanking me. In fact, every time she saw me, she thanked me. I eventually told her she didn't have to keep thanking me; I was just being obedient to God.

But I quickly began to see that this car, being a newer

model, was a bit of a learning curve for them. They were not used to so many gadgets and gizmos. The wife was completely overwhelmed, as she was the primary driver. I tried to explain certain of the car's features to her, and to help her in any way that I could. But I think that ultimately she felt overwhelmed by this newer car, and just felt more comfortable driving her older-model car (which she had already given away, or sold).

She eventually had a small fender-bender in the car. And it must have really shaken her up because she seemed to be afraid to drive the car after that. And not long after the accident, she decided to give up driving altogether. I was very sad to hear this because I knew that this meant a loss of her independence, which is something very hard for seniors to have to give up.

Through this experience, I began to see that sometimes we can even be overwhelmed by God's *blessings*. God clearly wanted me to bless them with this car, but the blessing was too much for them to handle. I was also feeling a little overwhelmed by my new car, too. It was more "fancy," and more powerful than anything

I had ever driven before. And in the beginning, I didn't want to drive it, preferring instead to drive my old car. But, I knew I had to get used to it. And as I continued to drive it, the more comfortable I felt in it, and I eventually began to love it. It just took some getting used to.

A lot of people want God to bless them—and bless them big! They want Him to open the windows of heaven, and pour out on them all of His blessings, to overflowing. But God knows that we are unable to handle all of His blessings. His blessings are often bigger and more complex than anything we can ever imagine. His blessings can far exceed even our greatest expectations. And if we are not spiritually mature, they can overwhelm us, and cause us to stumble. God would not put more of His blessings on us than we are able to handle.

With some people, if God were to bless them with $1 million today, they would probably be overwhelmed by so much money. But, this is often how we want God to bless us. But the truth of the matter is that if we have never been able to manage $100, that's a pretty good indicator that we would probably not be able to manage $1 million. And if we have not shown God that He can trust us with little, how do we expect Him to trust us with much?

God's blessings are not for us to spend satisfying all of our carnal desires. When God blesses us, He wants us to use it to be a blessing to others. Of course, He wants us to take care of our own needs, but more importantly, He wants us to care for the needs of others. But, if you are already thinking about all the things you can buy with $1 million, you are not ready to receive God's blessings. That $1 million might be the very thing to cause you to stumble, and turn away from God. God would not put more on us than we can bear.

I was very sad to hear that this older lady decided to stop driving, and that she was overwhelmed by her blessing. But, I received a very valuable lesson through this experience: God wants to bless us, but He will never put more on us than we are able to handle. Before we start praying for God to rain down His blessings on us, we need to make sure that we are in a position to handle everything God is capable of blessing us with, because if we are not, it could cause more harm than good.

God knows how much we can handle, and He knows when we are ready to receive the full measure of His blessings. And when we are faithful over little, He will begin to bless us with much.

My destiny is wrapped up in God. He has prepared for me a destiny, and a purpose. His plans for me far exceed anything I can ever think or imagine. When God blesses us, He blesses us big. But, He first wants to know that He can trust us with His blessings. And He wants to be ensured that we will remain faithful to Him and not become attached to the material things of this world, which will all eventually fade away. He wants to know that *we* trust Him, and that our love for Him is real. God wants to know that we will be wise stewards, faithfully managing all of the resources He gives us. And He wants to know that we will take what He has given us and be a blessing to those in need. When God knows that He can trust us, then will we begin to see Him open up the windows of heaven, and pour out on us all of His blessings. But until then, until we've proven ourselves to be trustworthy, we should not expect to receive "much" from God.

BIBLE STUDY AND REFLECTION

BIBLE STUDY & REFLECTION

1. Scripture Reading: Genesis 1,2,3

In the beginning, God created the heavens, the earth, man, and a vast assortment of animals. He fashioned all of creation in the way that He desired things to be, according to His will for creation. Everything was good and perfect. But something went terribly wrong.
Question: What happened? And what were the end results? And, is it possible for man to live today, in a fallen world, according to God's original plan for mankind? Please explain.

2. Scripture Reading: Exodus 23:1-33

Even in a fallen world, God offers protection from barrenness, miscarriages, sickness, and disease, if we would only serve Him and obey His commandments. **Question: Why do you think Israel was not able to remain faithful to God, and obey His commandments?**

3. Scripture Reading: Exodus 25,26,27

From the beginning, God has desired to dwell among man. He planted a garden and placed Adam and Eve there, where He communed with them regularly. And, God told Moses to take up a collection from Israel so that they could build a sanctuary where He would dwell among them. **Question: How does God dwell among us today? What "offering" can we give today in order to build a "sanctuary" for God to dwell among us?**

4. Scripture Reading: Exodus 32:1-35

Because there was sin in the camp it had to be dealt with swiftly, and in such a drastic way to prevent it from spreading, leading to further sin against God. **Question: We do not advocate violence, but if it is discovered that there is such corruptible sin in the camp (the church) today, what would be the best course of action to take to prevent it from spreading, which, if left unaddressed, could lead to the contamination and corruption of the entire church?**

5. Scripture Reading: Leviticus 26:1-46

God gave to Israel commandments and ordinances, which He expected them to follow. And He warned them that there were penalties for disobeying Him. Man is always breaking his promises to God. Yet, God is more righteous than we are; even though He punishes us for our disobedience, He never breaks His covenant with us. He will always honor His covenant, no matter what. **Question: Has there ever been a time when God kept a promise to you, even though you were disobedient to Him? Please explain.**

6. Scripture Reading: Deuteronomy 4,5,6

Moses reminds Israel of all that God has done for them, and encourages them to obey God, and to never forget His laws. He shows them how God's laws will help keep them holy, safe, and protected, and will prevent them from corrupting their good land. **Question: What can we do to make sure we always remember God's laws, and obey them? And how can we pass these things on to the next generation?**

7. Scripture Reading: Deuteronomy 8:1-20

Moses told Israel that God humbled them in the wilderness, testing them, to see if they would obey Him or not. And as we know all too well, Israel failed the test, miserably. **Question: During our personal times of testing, what are some things we can do that would help us remain faithful to God, not turning back to sin, and defiling ourselves?**

8. Scripture Reading: Psalm 1:1-6

It is never wise to take council from ungodly men. In order to stay firmly rooted and grounded in God we must keep His word foremost in our hearts, and meditate on it day and night. **Question: Describe a time(s) when you either sought, or heeded, the advice of ungodly men. What were the results of such consultations? How can you be sure that you are only following sound, sage advise?**

9. Scripture Reading: Psalm 91:1-16

There is safety and protection for those who love God and for those who remain safely shielded under His protective wings. Though disease, pestilence, and all of the evil schemes and plans of the wicked one seek to overtake you, it will not in any way harm you, as long as you are safely tucked under God's wings. **Question: Do you think it's possible for one who is fully submissive and obedient to God's will to be removed from under His protection? Please explain.**

10. Scripture Reading: Psalm 104:1-35

Man is the only part of God's creation that has ever rebelled against Him. All of His other creation reverences Him, and responds to His voice. The sun rises and sets at His command. The moon and the stars declare that He is God. Even the animals have not rebelled against God and turned against nature, to the abomination of

God, as man has. All of God's other creation still pays homage to Him, and trembles at His voice. **Question: Has there ever been a time in your Christian walk when you rebelled against God? What was the outcome, or lesson(s) learned?**

11. Scripture Reading: Jeremiah 7,8,9

Israel's continual rejection of the Lord really hurt and infuriated Him at the same time. Their refusal to put away their idols and turn to the Lord led to their punishment and banishment from the land God had promised them. God used other nations to punish Israel for their disobedience. **Question: Do you see any similarities between Israel and the church today?**

12. Scripture Reading: Ezekiel 1-5

God has always sent warnings and corrections through His prophets to encourage His people to turn back to Him and to warn them of His coming judgments should they not repent, and should they continue in their sins. But God told Ezekiel that if he failed to pass along His warnings to the people, and they do not repent, and they die, their blood would be upon his head. **Question: What are some ways God warns and chastises us today? And, does God still use prophets today to speak to His people?**

13. Scripture Reading: Matthew 5,6,7

Jesus spent a good amount of time with His disciples, teaching them, and imparting into them His wisdom. Jesus knew the importance of impartation, and that His words were life to them. **Question: Today, what are some things we can do to ensure that the church is** being fed Jesus' life sustaining words?

14. Scripture Reading: Matthew 10:1-42

Jesus called His disciples together and gave them a mission. He gave them power over unclean spirits (to cast them out), and power to heal every kind of sickness and disease. He told them to preach the gospel to the lost, and to not seek to acquire money or material possessions for their service. He warned them that the road would be hard, but those who endured to the end would be saved. **Question: The church also has a mission from the Lord. What do you think our mission is today; and is it similar to the mission Jesus gave His disciples, or have we been given a different mission?**

15. Scripture Reading: Matthew 14:13-36

Jesus displayed great faith when He fed a multitude of 5,000 with two fish and five loaves of bread. His faith was also on display when He walked on the water, and when He calmed the raging sea. **Question: This was all clearly a miracle; and a miracle is something that cannot be explained. But, based on what we know about Jesus' miracle-working power, first of all, do you believe in His power? And, do you believe that Jesus is able to perform a miracle in your life today?**

16. Scripture Reading: Matthew 24,25

Jesus gave His disciples certain signs to look for that point to His return, and the end of the world. He told them to always be watchful and to expect His return at any moment, because no one knows the exact day or the hour when He will return. **Question: What are you doing in preparation for Jesus' return?**

17. Scripture Reading: Matthew 26:1-75

Judas Iscariot betrayed Jesus for thirty pieces of silver. And Peter denied that he was one of His followers when he saw that Jesus was about to be tried and crucified. **Question: Has there ever been a time when you denied, or were ashamed to admit that you were a Christian (a follower of Jesus)? Please explain.**

18. Scripture Reading: Matthew 27,28

Jesus suffered many things at the hands of wicked men during His time on earth, all of which He endured with grace and dignity, never wavering one moment from His mission. And when their hatred of Jesus became so great, they crucified Him like a common thief. But, had He not died and rose again on the third day there would be no hope for the redemption of lost humanity, nor would He have been rewarded with all-power and authority by the Father. **Question: We have heard of** many believers in times past, and even today, who have suffered a fate similar to Jesus' at the hands of wicked men. And Jesus said that those who would be His disciples should be prepared to suffer along with Him. **Are you also as devoted to Jesus that you are prepared to suffer, and perhaps die for Him? (This may be something you need to take some time to think about.)**

19. Scripture Reading: John 20,21

Jesus showed Himself to His disciples after His resurrection. He showed them His nailed-scarred hands, and His side, proving to them who He was, and that He had in fact risen from the dead as He said He would. Once they had seen the physical signs, they believed, Thomas included. **Question: This is more a question for reflection: Do you sometimes find yourself doubting your faith, struggling to comprehend the existence of**

God (an invisible God), whom you've never seen?

20. Scripture Reading: Acts 17:1-15

This particular Scripture has become one of my guiding principles. The people of Berea set an example for all of us to follow. When Paul and Silas came to them preaching the word of God, they readily received it with joy, and began to search the Scriptures daily to see if those things they preached were true. In other words, they didn't just take Paul and Silas' word for it; they delved into the Scriptures for themselves, seeking further clarity and insight into the Scriptures. **Reflection: I would also like to encourage you to follow the Bereans' example. When you hear something—whether it's on Christian television, or even preached across the pulpit—don't just take their word for it, but study the word for yourself. Search the Scriptures daily to find out whether those things are truth. Ask God to open up the**

Scriptures to you, and pray for revelation. "Blessed are they which do hunger and thirst after righteousness: for they shall be filled."

21. Scripture Reading: Romans 8:1-39

As Christians, we have a responsibility to walk after the leading of the Spirit putting to death the flesh, not being led by it's sinful cravings. The effects of sin can be seen in our mortal bodies, which decay and eventually die. Its effects can also be seen in all of nature (Creation), which is groaning out for the redemption of God's children, which will also set it (Creation) free from its curse and restore it back to its glory days, prior to the fall of man. **Question: What parameters can you put in place to make sure that you are not being ruled by your sinful flesh, but are being led by and controlled by God's Spirit?**

22. Scripture Reading: Romans 12,13

The transformation that takes place in a person who is born-again, and who is full of the Holy Ghost, should reflect in his or her relationship with God, and in their relationship with their fellow man. This transformation starts on the inside and will inevitably be reflected on the outside. When God changes us, we no longer conform to the world's evil standards and dictates, but are changed, reflecting God's holy principles and standards, which now guide us. **Question: Are you living a life, today, that is being guided by God's holy principles and standards? If not, what are some things you plan to do to make sure your life conforms to God's standards of holiness?**

23. Scripture Reading: Ephesians 1,2,3

Here, we find a powerful and enlightening prayer that Paul routinely prayed over the church at Ephesus (see,

1:15-23). This is also my prayer for you: That God would grant you a spirit of wisdom and revelation (insight into the mysteries and secrets) in the deep and intimate knowledge of Him. That your heart would be flooded with light so that you can know and understand the hope to which He has called you, and how rich is His glorious inheritance in the saints. And, that you can know and understand what is the immeasurable and unlimited and surpassing greatness of His power in and for us who believe, as demonstrated in the working of His mighty strength, which He exerted in Christ when He raised Him from the dead, and seated Him at His own right hand in the heavenly places. May Christ, through your faith, forever dwell in your hearts. And may you be rooted deep in love, and may your foundation be securely established on love. And finally, may you come to know, through experience, the love of Christ, which far surpasses mere knowledge, without experience. And that you may be filled up in your being with all of the fullness of God, becoming wholly filled and flooded with God Himself in your inner man. Amen (so be it).

24. Scripture Reading: 1 Thessalonians 4,5

We are reminded that we should always be alert, looking for and expecting Christ's return. Because no man knows the day or the hour when Jesus will return for His church, we should always be ready and watchful, discerning the times. The church should be praying unceasingly, building up one another in our faith, and looking for that blessed day when Jesus will return rescuing us from this world and taking us to our heavenly home where we will live with Him for an eternity. (Comfort one another with these words.)

25. Scripture Reading: Titus 1,2,3

Paul reminds Titus of how those who are in the faith should conduct themselves: They should be firmly rooted in sound doctrine. They should be above reproach. They should not be busybodies, meddling in the affairs of others. But they should work diligently with their hands, taking care of their families, and engaging in good deeds to help meet the needs of others. **Reflection: This would be a good time for you to reflect on your life. Do you feel that you are firmly rooted in sound doctrine (standing firmly on God's word)? And, do you feel you are living a life that God would approve of? What are you doing right? Are there any areas where you are lacking? If so, what are you planning to do differently moving forward?**

26. Scripture Reading: Hebrews 11:1-40

Faith is the physical, tangible evidence of the things we are hoping for. Although we can not see it with our physical eyes, we can, however, see it by faith. And, although we can't touch it with our physical hands, we can touch it with faith. **Reflection: When we have faith, we are completely convinced that the things we are hoping for will happen, and will start making** preparations for them because we believe it's only a matter of time before they manifest themselves. Faith is the <u>evidence</u> that the things we are hoping for are <u>real</u>. But, if we are not fully convinced, and are in any way doubtful, that tiny bit of doubt is enough to block it from manifesting itself into our reality. If you were truly convinced of something, why wouldn't you begin to prepare for it? The conviction alone would force you to take action.

27. Scripture Reading: 1 John 1-5

If we say that we love God, we should: follow after Him, keep His commandments, love our brother, give to those in need; and we would not love the world, or deny that Jesus is the Christ, or dwell outside of Him, or commit sin. **Question: If we say that we love God but we do not abide by any of these things, what are we?**

28. Scripture Reading: Revelation 1,2,3

This is worth taking a moment to reflect on. The Lord tells John to record the vision he sees in a book; and the mysteries contained in the prophecy, given to John in the vision, are to be read, heard, and kept by the seven churches: Ephesus, Smyrna, Pergamos, Thyatira, Sardis, Philadelphia, and Laodicea.

To the church of *Ephesus*, John writes, "you have left your first love (the Lord). Repent, and turn back to me."

To the church of *Smyrna,* he writes, "I know your affliction, your suffering, and your poverty. Remain loyally faithful unto death and I will give you the crown of life."

To the church of *Pergamos,* he writes, "You live in the midst of wickedness (Satan's throne), yet you did not deny me or deny your faith. Yet, there are some among you who are clinging to the teachings of Baalam, and the Nicolaitans. These people are to repent, or else I will fight against them with the sword of my mouth."

To the church of *Thyatira,* he writes, "I know your record of love, faith, service, and patient endurance. But, you tolerate Jezebel (that wicked idolatrous). I will destroy her and all those who follow her, unless they turn away from following her, and repent. But to the rest of you in Thyatira, hold fast until I come."

To the church of *Sardis,* he writes, "You are supposed to be alive, but you are dead. Rouse yourselves and keep awake, and strengthen and invigorate what remains and is on the point of dying. For I have not found any work of yours meeting the requirements of my God, or perfect in His sight. If you will not rouse yourselves and keep awake and watch, I will come upon you as a thief, and you will not suspect what hour I will come. But those of you who have not soiled their clothes, shall walk in white garments and I will not erase or blot out his name from the *Book of Life.* I will acknowledge him as mine and will confess his name openly before my Father and before His angels."

To the church of *Philadelphia,* he writes, "I know that you have but little power, and yet you have kept my word and guarded my message, and have not renounced or denied my name. Because of this, I will keep you safe from the hour of testing and will set an open door before you, which no one is able to shut. I am coming quickly: hold fast what you have so that no one may rob you and deprive you of your crown."

And finally, to the church of *Laodicea,* he writes, "You are neither cold or hot. Because you are lukewarm, I will vomit you out of my mouth. You have said, 'I am rich and have prospered in wealth, and am in need of nothing.' Yet you do not realize and understand that you are wretched, pitiable, poor, blind, and naked. I counsel you to purchase from me spiritual wealth, that you may be truly wealthy, and robed in white garments, and that your spiritual eyes may be opened. Those whom I love, I tell their faults and convict, convince, reprove, and chasten. So, be enthusiastic and burning with zeal, and repent. Behold, I stand at the door and knock, if any one hears and listens to and heeds my voice and opens the door, I will come in to him and will eat with him, and he will eat with me."

He who is able to hear, let him listen to and heed what the Spirit says to the churches.

Reflection: Although there are many schools of thought as to the interpretation of this book of Revelations (i.e. whether the prophecies contained in the book have already taken place, or are a foreshadowing of things to come, or are figurative or literal in nature.), what we do know is that God has always forewarned His people and given them plenty of time to change their ways before He administered His judgments for their sins. What we can infer from the first three chapters of this book is that God has some *concerns* about the conditions, attitudes, and the goings-on in these seven churches specifically. He also acknowledges that they are doing some things right, and praises them for these things. This clearly shows us that God actively monitors His people, correcting us when we go astray, praising us when we do well, and even punishing us when we refuse to repent from our wickedness and turn back to Him. He says that those who overcome and hold on and endure to the end will be granted a seat in His kingdom and their names will not be blotted out of the *Book of Life*. But those who refuse to heed His warnings, repent, and turn away from sin, will be punished with eternal flames. I strongly believe that Jesus is soon to come, and that God wants to make sure that we are ready for His return. He's trying to get our attention, to wake us out of our sleep, or stupor, and remind us to be watchful and ready when Jesus returns. The church may have become lax in our commitment to Him, and have shifted off into other things. But, it's time for us to return to our first love, remain committed to Him, and keep our garments unspotted from sin. Jesus is on His way back and we need to be alert and watchful and busy making preparations for His return. When He returns, will He find you asleep, or will He find you fully awake and eagerly awaiting His arrival? Be ready; He's coming soon!

RESOURCES

BIBLES

The Amplified Bible. Grand Rapids, MI: Zondervan Publishing House, 1987.

The Holy Bible: King James Version. Nashville, TN: Thomas Nelson Publishers, 1976.

New American Standard Bible. The MacArthur Study Bible. John MacArthur. Nashville, TN: Thomas Nelson Publishers, 2006.

BIBLE CONCORDANCE

The New Strong's Concordance of the Bible. James Strong, LL.D, S.T.D. Nashville, TN: Thomas Nelson Publishers, 1996.

DICTIONARIES

American Dictionary Of The English Language. Noah Webster, LL.D. Facsimile of 1st ed. New York: Foundation For American Christian Education, 1828.

The Compact Bible Dictionary. Grand Rapids, MI: Zondervan Publishing House, 1967.

The HarperCollins Bible Dictionary. Paul J. Achtemeier. Revised ed. San Francisco, CA: HarperOne, 1996.

Merriam-Webster's Collegiate Dictionary. 11th ed. Springfield, MA: Merriam-Webster, 2011.

The Student Bible Dictionary. Karen Dockery, Johnnie Godwin, Phyllis Godwin. Uhrichsville, OH: Barbour Books, 2000.

BOOKS

The Awakening in Wales: A First-hand Account of the Welsh Revival of 1904. Jessie Penn-Lewis. Fort Washington, PA: CLC Publications, 2012.

Azusa Street: An Eyewitness Account. Frank Bartleman. Centennial ed. Gainesville, FL: Bridge-Logos, 1980.

Azusa Street Mission And Revival: The Birth of the Global Pentecostal Movement. Cecil M. Robeck, Jr. Nashville, TN: Thomas Nelson, Inc., 2006.

The Gingerbread Man. Parragon Books, 2012.

Jewish Culture And Customs: A Sampler of Jewish Life. Steve Herzig. Bellmawr, NJ: The Friends of Israel Gospel Ministry, Inc., 1997.

The Welsh Revival. Reprint of the Narratives of W.T. Stead and G. Campbell Morgan. Boston: The Pilgrim Press, 1905.

ONLINE RESOURCES

Bible Gateway. biblegateway.com

Dictionary.com

Wikipedia: The Free Encyclopedia. wikipedia.org

NAYLA BOOK PUBLISHERS

Thank you for purchasing this book. We pray that you have been blessed by it.

More from Jeanita:

An Open Letter to the Church:
On Faith, Holiness, and Being
Full of the Holy Ghost

The Purpose of Man

Step Out of the Shadows:
Helping Widows Move Past Grief

Website:
naylabookpublishers

Contact:
info@naylabookpublishers.com

www.ingramcontent.com/pod-product-compliance
Lightning Source LLC
Chambersburg PA
CBHW022103290426
44112CB00008B/537